I AM ACE

of related interest

Ace and Aro Journeys
A Guide to Embracing Your Asexual or Aromantic Identity
The Ace and Aro Advocacy Project
ISBN 978 1 83997 638 4
eISBN 978 1 83997 639 1

How to Be Ace
A Memoir of Growing Up Asexual
Rebecca Burgess
ISBN 978 1 78775 215 3
eISBN 978 1 78775 216 0

How to Understand Your Sexuality
A Practical Guide for Exploring Who You Are
Meg-John Barker, Alex Iantaffi and Jules Scheele
ISBN 978 1 78775 618 2
eISBN 978 1 78775 619 9

Ace Voices
What it Means to Be Asexual, Aromantic, Demi or Grey-Ace
Eris Young
ISBN 978 1 78775 698 4
eISBN 978 1 78775 699 1

Sounds Fake But Okay
An Asexual and Aromantic Perspective on Love,
Relationships, Sex, and Pretty Much Anything Else
Sarah Costello and Kayla Kaszyca
ISBN 978 1 83997 001 6
eISBN 978 1 83997 002 3

I AM ACE

ADVICE ON LIVING YOUR BEST ASEXUAL LIFE

CODY DAIGLE-ORIANS

Jessica Kingsley Publishers
London and Philadelphia

First published in Great Britain in 2023 by Jessica Kingsley Publishers
An imprint of Hodder & Stoughton Ltd
An Hachette UK Company

1

A CIP catalogue record for this title is available from the British Library and
the Library of Congress

ISBN 978 1 83997 262 1
eISBN 978 1 83997 263 8

Printed and bound in the United States by Integrated Books International

Jessica Kingsley Publishers' policy is to use papers that are natural, renewable
and recyclable products and made from wood grown in sustainable forests.
The logging and manufacturing processes are expected to conform to the
environmental regulations of the country of origin.

Jessica Kingsley Publishers
Carmelite House
50 Victoria Embankment
London EC4Y 0DZ

www.jkp.com

This book is dedicated to my chosen family.
For Neil, who teaches me what unconditional love looks like.
For Scott, who shows me the universe is full of new possibilities.
For Daniel, who reminds me that joy can be found in everything.

This book came to be as we formed our constellation.
I wrote it by the light from your stars.

CONTENTS

CONTENTS

INTRODUCTION

If you're reading this book, we have something in common.

At some point, we both have asked ourselves, "Am I asexual?" For me, the answer to that question was "Yes!" and it led me down an eventful road that brought me a truckload of other questions, a lot of surprising answers, new relationships, new ways of seeing myself, new communities to find myself in, new ways of advocating for those communities, opportunities to educate, opportunities to learn, a lot of joy, and a tiny sliver of internet popularity.

Oh, and this book.

This book is the book I wish I had when I was 18 years old, confused about what I was feeling without the words to properly express it, knowing I was different but feeling lost in understanding it.

This is the book I wish I had when I was struggling in my twenties, through bad relationship after bad relationship, not understanding why sex and intimacy were so difficult for me, not understanding why I felt completely broken.

This is the book I wish I had when, in my thirties, my husband and I were hitting roadblocks in our relationship, feeling as though sometimes we couldn't fundamentally understand each other, as though we didn't really know who the other person was.

This is the book I wish I had when, in my early forties, I discovered

I was asexual, wanting a resource that simply answered my pressing questions and was an encouraging friend saying, "You've got this! You can do it! Go out there and be the best ace you can be!"

This book is for all of those versions of me.

And this book is for you, my unknown friend out there with questions of your own. I don't know where the question "Am I asexual?" is going to lead you, but I know it's probably led you here. I hope you find what you're looking for in these pages, and I hope what you encounter here encourages you to keep asking questions and keep on learning.

This book is divided into three parts

The first part, "Asexuality and You," covers the basics of your personal relationship to asexuality. We'll explore what asexuality is and how it works. We'll get a handle on the language of asexuality and how you might use it. And we'll talk about the challenges of accepting your asexuality—if that's what you want to do—and learn some strategies to make that process easier.

The second part, "Asexuality and Others," covers the ways we share our asexuality with other people. We'll talk about why and how to come out as asexual. We'll talk about how asexuality fits into relationships and how we can build fulfilling bonds with partners of all kinds. And we'll learn how to deal with some of the negative ideas other people have about asexuality and how to prevent them from holding you back.

The third part, "Asexuality and the World," explores how asexuality interacts with the rest of the world. We'll look at how asexuality fits into the LGBTQIA+ community. We'll learn about some of the powerful social constructs in which asexuality exists. And we'll bring it all together with a discussion about finding joy in our asexuality.

Will this book answer all of your questions about asexuality? Probably not. Asexuality is not a simple experience. Not only are there many different ways to be asexual, but your experience of asexuality will be different depending on who else you are in the world. The other experiences you inhabit—your experience of race, of gender, of your culture or religion, of your socioeconomic background, whether or not you're disabled, whether or not you're neurodivergent—will impact how you experience asexuality and how your asexuality is treated.

This book can't account for every ace's experience, and I, as its author, can't speak for every ace person. What I and this book have attempted to do, however, is tackle the basic questions that many of us face at the start of our journeys and provide a jumping off point for you to dig deeper into the complexities of the ace experience with other books, authors, and activists. If you don't totally see yourself in this book, that's okay. Take what's useful. Discard what's not. There are many more ace folks out there writing, thinking, and creating about the ace experience. You will find your reflection in them even if you don't necessarily find it here.

If we're all setting foot into the dark woods of the ace experience, I hope you see this book less as a map and more as a flashlight.

Let's go.

PART I

Asexuality and You

Chapter 1

WHAT IS ASEXUALITY?
UNDERSTANDING ORIENTATION

I didn't always know I was asexual. In fact, I spent almost all of my life thinking I wasn't. (I didn't come out as asexual until I was 42. More on that experience later.) From the time I started feeling the first little sparks of attraction in middle school until a third of the way through my fourth decade on the planet, I was searching for the right words to describe me.

When I was a teenager, I was incredibly confused about sex. Everything about it—how it worked, *why* it worked, how you decided you wanted to do it, how you found someone to do it with, what the rules were, how you even learned the rules, how all of that complexity related to me—seemed impossibly out of reach. It was a secret language I hadn't learned how to speak, an exclusive club I wasn't invited to join.

I knew that I was attracted to other boys. *That* was clear to me. I owned that. I would never say it out loud, for fear of being picked on, beaten up, or worse by the boys I was feeling those feelings for. But I knew that I was attracted to them.

At least, I *assumed* I was attracted to them. I liked looking at them. I liked watching them move through halls between classes, goofing

around, shoving each other, and laughing. I liked watching them in
P.E., doing warmups, playing whatever sport they were good at and I
wasn't. I liked watching them slouch in their desks in class, bored and
totally over algebra or geography, chewing on a pen cap or doodling on
a notebook. I felt drawn to them, their bodies, the way they moved, the
way they wore their clothes, the way they occupied space. I wanted to
be close to them, hang out with them, and be accepted by them.

And sometimes, I really wanted to cuddle up next to them, too.
This only happened with the boys I developed real friendships with.
I'd imagine what it would feel like to sit next to them on a couch and
watch a movie, snuggled up next to each other. I'd imagine what it
would feel like to be in their bed, holding them or being held by them,
falling asleep, listening to them breathe. I'd imagine a world where the
space they inhabited was one I was invited into and was made to feel
like it was my space, too.

I didn't want to have sex with them, though. That never really
crossed my mind. Or if it did cross my mind—because I knew that it
should; it was crossing the minds of everyone else I knew, so I assumed
it should be crossing mine as well—it just seemed like a weird thing to
do. I couldn't make the mental leap from that safe, inviting cuddling
space to sex. It wasn't something I felt a strong desire to engage in. And
most of the time, I couldn't even imagine what I would be doing if I did.
I was attracted to boys, but I suppose I wasn't *attracted* attracted.

I was attracted to girls, too, but in a very different way. I was more
drawn to girls romantically. It was easy for me to develop crushes on
girls in my classes, easy to develop close friendships with them. As
much as it would get me picked on by the boys (and always by the boys
I most wanted to watch and touch), I took every opportunity I could
to hang out with and build bonds with the girls. There would be one
or two who would really get those warm, squishy feelings going in me,
and those feelings would flood my brain the more I'd spend time with
them. I'd want to plan dates with them, be their boyfriend, perform
romantic gestures for them, and live out every romantic movie trope

I could think of. I wanted to love them, as much as I knew what that meant. And I wanted them to love me back.

But I didn't want to have sex with them, either. I'd get very nervous any time the possibility of physical intimacy would come up with one of the girls I dated. It was just like it was with boys. I either never thought about it or my brain would get stuck and not be able to take the leap to even *imagine* what physical intimacy would be like. Even with the one girl I had a very serious relationship with—a girl I was starting to see as my potential wife, a woman I'd want to spend the rest of my life with—I couldn't, no matter how close we got, really imagine having sex with her. We could do everything else. But sex...

I guess I wasn't *attracted* attracted to girls, either.

I wanted boys, but I also wanted girls. I wanted them, but I wanted them very differently. I wanted some kinds of closeness, but I didn't want sex. I knew everyone around me was obsessed with sex, thought about it all the time, talked about it endlessly, but I didn't understand why. They were all experiencing lust and want and a high-grade, persistent horniness. I was experiencing confusion and anxiety and a low-grade, persistent feeling that something was really, really wrong with me. We were all going through the madness and chaos of adolescence, but for some reason, my madness and chaos were completely different from everyone else's.

There was a word for the chaos I was experiencing: asexuality. But I didn't have that word yet. I didn't have access to it. I didn't see it represented in any books or movies or TV shows. I didn't see it modeled in any of the people I knew. I couldn't go to Tumblr and check out some posts about it, because Tumblr didn't exist, and I'm old enough to have gone through almost my whole high school experience without the internet at all.

So, I decided I was gay. It was close to what I was feeling, and I felt comfortable claiming it. I assumed maybe my romantic feelings about girls were just wishful thinking, and that even though I didn't really want to have sex with anyone, cuddling with guys was enough to qualify me for homosexuality. It still wasn't right, but I felt I had no other choices.

I settled for words and identities that didn't quite fit. They were close, but not exactly right.

They spoke to some of the story of me, but not all of it.

That may be where you are now. You might be experiencing some madness and chaos of your own when it comes to sex and attraction. Sex might seem confusing and incomprehensible. It might be the source of a lot of anxiety or fear. You might be feeling left out or like you're falling behind. Worst of all, you might be feeling a little broken.

You may be using language that doesn't quite fit, words to describe who you are that tell only half of your story. Or maybe you haven't found the right words to describe you. Maybe you haven't found any language at all that speaks to what you live each day.

This chapter will be a first step in sorting some of that out. We are going to talk about sexual orientation: what it is, what the spectrum of orientations looks like, and how asexuality fits into that spectrum.

What is asexuality?

Let's go right to the big question: What is asexuality?

Asexuality is a sexual orientation that includes any person who does not experience or rarely experiences sexual attraction.

This definition seems pretty simple in theory, right? In practice, however, this definition creates a big tent, describing a diverse spectrum of experiences, a wide range of relationships to sex and intimacy, and a vibrant community containing people from all walks of life.

To really understand asexuality—and to see if asexuality describes your experience—we have to break down this simple definition, explore its component parts, and expand our ideas about sex, intimacy, and attraction.

What is sexual orientation?

Asexuality is a sexual orientation. So, let's start by breaking down what that means.

Sexual orientation takes a big-picture look at how you, as an individual, relate to sexual attraction over time. If you're reading this book, you've probably been thinking a lot about this relationship. It can be overwhelming trying to sort out the complicated and conflicting feelings we have about attraction: Is this sexual attraction? Is this some other kind of attraction? Will these feelings change down the road? Have my real feelings even started happening yet? Do I even know what I'm feeling and experiencing in the first place?

For our purposes, we'll focus on three key things that help us identify our sexual orientation. First, sexual orientation describes an innate relationship we have to sexual attraction. Second, it describes a pattern of experience we have of sexual attraction throughout our lives. And finally, it describes the gender or genders you feel sexual attraction to.

Some definitions of sexual orientation are more expansive than this and include your romantic or emotional attractions. Those definitions include these things because, for most people, the different attractions they experience all point in the same direction. They experience sexual, emotional, and romantic attraction for the same kind of person in the same kind of way for most of their lives. But as we will explore later when we look deeper into how attraction works, this isn't the reality for everyone. I want to keep things clear and focused, so in our discussion, sexual orientation describes the specifics of sexual attraction only.

Sexual orientation is innate

Most people, when they think about their sexual orientation, think of it as something that comes from someplace deep inside them. It's a feeling that's always been there. It's a thing they discover or recognize about themselves, not something they decide. And this feeling, the innateness of sexual orientation, is felt by people of all sexual orientations. It's not specific to one or a few of them. Sexual orientation, regardless of how we identify, isn't just a choice we make or a phase we go through. It isn't imposed on us by others and it's not a result of our behaviors. It's part of how we're built. It's fundamental to who we are. You can think of sexual orientation as your "factory settings."

This is a helpful starting place to think about your own sexual orientation. What feelings about sex and attraction feel deeply a part of you? What feelings feel as though they've always been there? What are the feelings that can't get swept aside or decided away into oblivion? Those feelings are where we can begin to look for clarity on sexual orientation.

Now, when you dig into queer theory and other academic thought about gender and sexuality, along with some crowded corners of discourse on the internet, you will find people saying that sexual orientation isn't innate. Most often, you'll find arguments that "it's complicated"—that sexual orientation is a mixture of innate feeling and environmental influence—but you'll also find arguments that you *can* just choose your orientation. All of this is fair and valid. Human sexuality is extremely complex, and the deeper you dive into the thinking, writing, and research on it, the more complex it reveals itself to be. But most people, particularly people who are in the early parts of figuring out their relationship to their own sexuality, aren't swimming in that deep end of the theory pool. They're *feeling* their orientation, not *thinking* about it. And most people, regardless of where they land on the orientation spectrum, experience sexual orientation as something deeply rooted, original, and not a choice.

Sexual orientation is a pattern of experience

While our relationship to sex and attraction may not always be the most reliable or predictable, we can often take a step back from a moment-to-moment survey of our feelings and find some patterns in our overall experience. We can see that certain things happen again and again. Or we can see that certain things are missing again and again. Those patterns, those repeated motifs in the sum of our experience, are helpful in clarifying our sexual orientation.

Our sexual orientation is not the product of a single encounter or a single feeling. It's not determined by any one point on your timeline. It expresses your repeated experience over time. For many people, figuring out their sexual orientation is a bit like putting together a jigsaw puzzle. It's not simply zeroing in on a single piece. It's the process of putting many pieces, many similar experiences and feelings, together and coming up with one complete picture. The pattern is what makes your orientation.

What patterns exist in your experience around sex and attraction? Are you always attracted to one specific gender? Are you always attracted to a certain aesthetic style a person may have? When you feel attraction, do you always think about doing certain kinds of things with a person? Or is your pattern more about what's not there? Do you find yourself not feeling attracted to any kind of person? Do you find yourself only drawn to being friends or only drawn to holding hands at most? All of these patterns help define your orientation.

That isn't to say that these patterns must remain rigidly unchanging. Over the course of your life, you may find that your patterns of sexual attraction evolve and change. Sometimes, those changes are the result of you growing and changing as a person. Sometimes, those changes occur because of external forces. Trauma is a very common external force that can disrupt these patterns. Regardless of the reason, it's okay that some patterns end and new ones take their place. Change doesn't invalidate new patterns. Who you become doesn't invalidate who you were.

Gender helps define sexual orientation

Sexual orientation is described by the gender or genders of the people we are sexually attracted to. The direction of attraction is one of the important ways we define orientations, and the language we use to talk about sexual orientation focuses on gender.

Do you feel sexual attraction to people of a different gender to you or the same gender to you? Do you feel sexual attraction only to people of one gender or of many genders? Do you feel sexual attraction to no one, regardless of their gender? Does gender even matter at all when you're thinking about your sexual attraction? These questions help us match our experience to the language we have for sexual orientation, and they point us in the direction of the label that best suits us.

Is it a perfect system? No. Gender is as complicated an experience as sexual orientation, and for many people, their experience of gender brushes up against their experience of sexual orientation in ways that make both experiences more complicated. If the journey to fully understand your sexual orientation is intersecting with the journey to fully understand your gender identity, know that some of these questions may be harder to answer. Show yourself compassion. Give yourself grace. We don't have to have all the answers right now. We can make our best guesses. We can get comfortable in the uncertainty. And we can keep being curious, keep exploring, keep learning.

It would be wonderful to have a way to talk about sexual orientation that didn't rely so heavily on gender, especially when the Western understanding of gender is very binary. But, we have the language we have. So we'll do what we can to make the best of it.

What are the different sexual orientations?

Now we have the big picture of what sexual orientation is: the innate and enduring pattern of a person's experience of sexual attraction. From that big picture, things branch off in two main directions: allosexuality and asexuality.

Allosexuality is an umbrella term for all of the sexual orientations that regularly experience sexual attraction. A vast majority of people in the world are allosexual. Allosexuality is so common that it is considered the "default" human experience of sexual attraction. It's assumed that everyone is born allosexual, and any deviations from that norm are the result of some brokenness or incompleteness in a person.

This is not true. Allosexuality and the orientations that fall under its umbrella are just one part of the spectrum of human sexual identity.

There are many sexual orientations under the allosexual umbrella, but the five orientations that follow are the broadest and most commonly known orientations.

Heterosexuality is a sexual orientation that includes people who experience sexual attraction to people of a gender different from their own. Heterosexuality is usually culturally understood through the lens of the gender binary—that gender is simply male and female. While this isn't universally true for heterosexual people, when heterosexuality is considered, it's usually considered as "a man and a woman."

Homosexuality is a sexual orientation that includes people who experience sexual attraction to people of the same gender as their own. The experiences of gay and lesbian people are usually understood through the lens of the gender binary. While not universally true, when homosexuality is considered, it's usually considered as "a man and a man" or "a woman and a woman."

Bisexuality is a sexual orientation that includes people who experience sexual attraction to people of two or more genders. Older understandings of bisexuality were also focused on the gender binary, defining the orientation as being attracted to men and women. But the definition has evolved to refer to people who experience sexual attraction to more than one gender.

Pansexuality is a sexual orientation that includes people who experience sexual attraction to people without regard for their gender. Pansexual people are attracted to others of all genders, or they will say the gender of their partner does not play a role in their attraction to them. "Pansexual" is a nuanced term that a few short sentences cannot entirely contain.

Omnisexuality is a sexual orientation that includes people who experience attraction to people of all genders. For omnisexual people, the gender of their partner does play a role in their attraction to them, or they experience attraction to all genders, with some preferences. "Omnisexual" is sometimes used interchangeably with "pansexual," although not every person using the terms would agree. And "omnisexual" is also a nuanced term that a few short sentences cannot entirely contain.

In another part of the sexual orientation spectrum are those with orientations that don't experience or rarely experience sexual attraction: asexuality. According to research, approximately one percent of the world's population identifies somewhere on the asexual spectrum. And although the visible, vocal community of asexual individuals is relatively new, asexuality and asexual people have existed throughout history. Asexual people aren't deviations of allosexual people, nor are we broken versions of allosexuals. Asexuality is a natural, normal way to experience the world and is a valid relationship to sexual attraction.

Asexuality is a broad spectrum on its own, as we'll explore in the next chapter, containing many different identities and modes of asexual expression. The asexual spectrum contains a handful of identity labels that describe broad experiences of asexuality; a group of smaller, more specialized terms that represent more specific experiences within the asexual spectrum; and language for describing how asexual individuals, through their identities, relate to sexual activity.

So if I'm asexual, does that mean I don't have a sexual orientation?

No. Asexuality *is* a sexual orientation. It's not a lack or absence of one.

This is a common and pervasive misconception about asexuality: that not feeling or rarely feeling sexual attraction means a person doesn't possess something that other, "normal" people possess.

We will spend a lot of time in this book talking about cultural norms, cultural constructs, the messages of the dominant culture, and the stereotypes and untruths about asexuality we're taught from the time we're very young. And there's a thought that runs underneath all of those external forces: that if something is more common, that thing is more natural, more valid, more right.

This belief is false. Yes, more people in the world experience sexual attraction than not. But that fact doesn't make that experience a default. It doesn't make that experience right. And conversely, it doesn't make other, less common experiences deviations from a default. It doesn't make other, less common experiences wrong.

Not or rarely experiencing sexual attraction—asexuality—is not a broken version of another experience. It is not a state of missing something. It is not a lack of something everyone else possesses.

Asexuality is a sexual orientation. It is a natural, authentic way of experiencing the world. It is a whole experience in and of itself.

What if I'm still not sure what my sexual orientation is?

It's okay not to have it all figured out. We've all been there. A lot of us will end up there again.

It's okay to be confused, to feel like you don't fit in anywhere, to feel like you don't know yourself at all.

It's okay to take the dots in your life and connect them the wrong way for a while, to put the pieces together the wrong way, or to give your experience the wrong name.

It's okay not to know what to do, to feel like you don't have the right words.

It's okay to feel broken.

We're all there at some point.

We just have to remember that we never have to stay there. We can move. We can rearrange the pieces. We can reconnect the dots. We can find new words. We can grow out of one place and grow into another.

Chapter 2

WHAT IS ASEXUALITY?
UNDERSTANDING ATTRACTION

There were many things I loved about my first boyfriend, but what I loved most was that he had his own apartment.

That may seem callous. But I was 18 years old. I was just starting college, and I was still living at home, a concession I had made so I wouldn't have to get a job while going to school. Meeting him was exciting. He was the first honest-to-god gay guy I met after coming out as gay myself, and he was all the things I was looking for at the time. He was cute. He made me laugh. He gave incredible hugs. And although he was almost 6'5" tall and a big, broad-shouldered 280 pounds, he was one of the most gentle humans I'd ever met. He treated me with such care and kindness. I wanted to spend every spare moment I had with him. But I wasn't bringing this beautiful, benevolent behemoth back home to watch TV with my parents on a Friday night. That wasn't happening.

Thank god he had his own place. It wasn't much. I would say none of the furniture matched, but that would be overstating the presence of furniture in the first place. There was a couch and a TV on a couple of crates. A room lamp. His roommate's dining room table with some mismatched chairs. His bed was just a mattress and box spring on the floor shoved up against the wall. It was "minimalist," as a great generosity. But at least I could go there and be with him.

"So...what do you wanna do now?" he'd ask me as we cuddled on the couch. This would usually follow the end of some movie we'd picked for the night, a mostly devoured bowl of popcorn on the floor beside us, the room's lone floor lamp reduced to a soft, romantic glow.

"I dunno," I'd say. "We can do whatever."

"Whatever?" His voice would arch upward, making very clear that his list of options had been whittled down to one.

"Whatever," I'd say. "You know, I just like...relaxing with you."

Was I relaxed? Not even close. These moments were four-alarm fires in my brain. I was really into him. I wanted to be here, on this couch and in his arms. Being close to him, touching him, sharing his space was something I wanted, something I maybe craved. But I knew the "whatever" he wanted was sex, and that was something that scared me, that made me want to push away. I couldn't find sex in all the things I wanted with him, and I didn't understand why.

Maybe he's just not the right person, I thought. Maybe with someone else, you'll want that "whatever." Maybe with someone else, it'll be different. When my relationship with him ended, and I found myself on different couches at the end of different movies looking into the eyes of different guys who were asking, "So...what do you wanna do now?," the same four-alarm fires were blazing through my brain. The "whatever" was still sex, and no matter how well I hit it off with someone, no matter what connections were there, no matter what attractions sparked between us, I couldn't find sex in the things I wanted.

I expected the madness and chaos of high school to end once I'd made my mind up that I was gay. I had figured it out, right? I picked a team. All of this confusion and uncertainty was supposed to be gone now. But here it still was, and it was more confusing than ever. I'd find people I liked and who liked me back. We wanted each other, but why didn't I want in the same way they did? Wasn't it enough to find someone to want? Wasn't this feeling, this craving—to be close, to be intimate, to be body to body—the want that led to sex? What was wrong with me? Why couldn't I just be normal like them?

"Picking a team" didn't solve all my problems. Not only had I picked the wrong team, but I also didn't understand the mechanics of what made any of the teams a team in the first place.

I didn't understand attraction.

In this chapter, we're going to explore attraction: what it is, how it operates, and how it differs from things like arousal or libido. Understanding attraction will help us break down our own experiences and look at it more completely. And it will help us clarify our understanding of our sexual orientation.

What is sexual attraction?

We know sexual orientation is a description of a person's relationship to sexual attraction. But what is sexual *attraction*?

In broadest terms, sexual attraction is the attraction one feels, directed at a person or a kind of person, that makes one want to have sex.

It can be difficult to describe what sexual attraction feels like, especially for an asexual person who's never experienced it. And there are many different factors that influence sexual attraction. But at its core, it's an attraction that makes one want to engage in sexual activity. There can be variation in what those activities are, and there can be variation in who those activities are shared with. People will experience the physical specifics of sexual attraction in different ways. But if the want to have sex is there, it's probably sexual attraction.

Sexual attraction is also directional. It has a focus toward a person or a kind of person. This is one of the things that separate sexual attraction from arousal or libido. Attraction in all its forms moves in a particular direction: in the direction of a specific gender or genders, in specific aesthetic directions, or in specific emotional or intellectual directions. It's seeing that person who's "your type" and being drawn to them in a sexual way. It's feeling that pull to be sexual or experience something sexual in the specific direction of a person.

Let's think about it this way: If you're a radio, sexual attraction is your "song." It may contain the same notes and beats that everyone else's song does. But the arrangement is specific to you. Doesn't matter how loud or soft you play it, how fast or slow or often, your song is your song.

How does sexual attraction differ from sex drive or libido?

Sexual attraction is not the same thing as sex drive, or libido.

Like sexual attraction, libido is a desire or want to have sex. But unlike sexual attraction, libido is not directional. It isn't aimed at a particular person or kind of person. It's the more general desire to engage in sexual activity, to experience sexual pleasure.

Libido is what people are describing when they say they just need to "scratch that itch" or when they are feeling "horny." It's describing an unspecific desire to have sex. Sometimes that desire can be really strong—a high libido. Sometimes that desire can be much lower, like background noise—a low libido. You can think of libido like volume settings, describing the general intensity of sexual desire rather than its innate direction.

I'll share with you my favorite analogy about the difference between sexual attraction and libido. I like it because it's clear and concise. I also like it because it's about food.

Sexual attraction is like being hungry for pizza. You know you're hungry, and you know exactly what you're hungry for. You don't want hamburgers. You don't want tacos. You want pizza. Your hunger has a direction, and that direction is the nearest Domino's.

Libido is like just being generally hungry. You know you want to eat something, but you're not sure what. If you had a pizza, that would be fine. But if you just had trail mix, that would be fine, too. You would also be fine if you didn't eat anything. It's hunger without a direction, and it would just be cooler if you had a snack.

Libido doesn't figure into sexual orientation in the way that attraction does. In fact, libido operates separately from sexual orientation. Allosexual people can have low or no libido. Asexual people can have a very high libido. The intensity of one's sex drive doesn't define how they identify. And, consequently, how one chooses to act on their libido doesn't define how they identify, either.

Okay, but what about arousal? What's that?

See how this can get complicated really quickly?

Arousal is the feeling of your body and your mind being stimulated, awakened, "on." This is both a physical experience and a mental one, and in this context, it's the physical and mental experience of being awakened or turned on in a sexual way.

Arousal, libido, and sexual attraction can seem like three different words for the same basic idea. That overlap among them can be very confusing for ace folks at the beginning of their journeys. If the terms are all speaking about the same thing, how do you know which one you're experiencing and—more frustratingly—how can you tell which ones you're not experiencing?

While they do cover similar ground, sexual attraction, libido, and arousal are all very specific experiences. Here's a good way to think about those differences.

Arousal is a "right now" experience. It's happening in your body and in your mind at this moment, and it's tied to this moment. It's a response to some kind of stimulus—visual, tactile, verbal, fantasized— or, sometimes, it's just a response that shows up all on its own.

Libido is more about intensity and frequency. Libido is a way to think about how often arousal happens for you and whether it's really intense or more low-key. While arousal is generally a response to a stimulus, libido describes the qualities of those responses in you.

Sexual attraction is concerned with direction—*where* is your libido going? *Who* is your libido focused on? If you're allosexual, these questions have pretty clear answers. If you're asexual, things might be a little foggier.

For the average allosexual person, these three things work harmoniously and effortlessly together, so much so that allosexual folks rarely even think about these distinctions at all. But as soon as these three experiences stop working in such harmony, things get confusing, and they get there fast. Knowing these distinctions becomes enormously helpful to understanding your experience.

You can experience some of these but not all of them. You can experience none of them. They can all be present but operate on different wavelengths. All of these things are possible. But none of these variations mean that you're broken or that something is wrong with the way you're wired.

Variation is natural.

So if I'm asexual, can I experience any attraction at all?

In short: absolutely.

Asexuality, like most queer identities, sits in a strange place culturally. Because such a small percentage of people in the world are asexual, and because there is so little information and representation of asexuality circulating in the mainstream culture, most people know more asexual stereotypes than asexual truths. One of the most common stereotypes about asexuality is that being asexual means you experience no attraction at all.

The mainstream image of the asexual person is of a human blank slate, a person who doesn't want sex, who doesn't want relationships, who doesn't feel desire, who doesn't feel love. Asexual people are believed to be islands within themselves, absent of human connection.

This is, of course, absurd. Not experiencing sexual attraction doesn't mean you abdicate all forms of human connection. It just means you don't experience sexual attraction. But there is a dominant cultural idea about sex and attraction that makes separating sexual attraction from other kinds of attraction very difficult.

We think about sex and attraction—and all the ways you can be into another person—as being interconnected. We imagine them arriving all wrapped up together. As far as the dominant culture goes, sex and attraction of any kind are symbiotic. You can't have one without the other.

What this leads to is the belief that any feeling of interest, of *attraction*, is the same thing. If someone's cute, that means you want to have sex with them. And if you're attracted to them sexually, you will want to emotionally connect with them. And if you can emotionally connect with them, that likely means there's potential for you to date and/or marry them.

See the problem?

In reality, attraction isn't just one thing. It's many things. There are many ways to be attracted to a person. And each kind of attraction is its own thing. They exist separately. They work independently.

You can think someone's cute but not be sexually attracted to them.

You can want to have sex with someone and have no romantic interest in them at all.

You can have deep romantic feelings about someone but not be sexually attracted to them.

This dominant cultural misconception about the interconnectedness of attraction is what makes asexuality confusing to some people. When we say "I don't experience sexual attraction," what people often hear in their mind is "I'M NOT ATTRACTED TO ANYTHING EVER FOR ALL OF TIME!"

And that's just not true. Asexual individuals don't experience *one* kind of attraction. That's it. We can—and often do—experience the others.

What are the different kinds of attraction?

Sexual attraction isn't the only game in town when it comes to attraction. There are many other ways we can be attracted to other people.

Romantic attraction is an attraction to a person or a kind of person that makes you want to pursue romantic relationships with them.

Aesthetic attraction is an attraction to the way a person looks, the way they carry themselves, or the visual aesthetic they cultivate. This attraction doesn't, however, make one inclined to pursue physical or sexual contact.

Emotional attraction is an attraction to a person or a kind of person that makes you want to establish deep connections or emotional bonds with them. This attraction doesn't, however, make one inclined to pursue something sexual or romantic.

Sensual attraction is an attraction to a person or a kind of person that makes you want to share physical closeness or non-sexual physical intimacy with them. Things like cuddling, kissing, holding hands, and hugging can be ways to express sensual attraction.

Intellectual attraction is an attraction to the way a person thinks or the way they engage with ideas. Having a desire to "get inside their head" or to engage in challenging conversation with someone are ways to express intellectual attraction.

Alterous attraction is an attraction to a person or a kind of person that makes you want to develop a deep, connected relationship with them that's somewhere between romantic and platonic.

These aren't the only types of attractions that human beings can experience. But even this representative sample shows you how varied human connection can be. Being asexual doesn't cut you off from all of these other attractions. You can experience all of these, some of these, or none of these as an asexual person. What's important is understanding that all of these attractions operate on their own. How we experience one doesn't determine how we experience the others.

The split-attraction model

Some individuals on the asexual spectrum use the split-attraction model to help understand and explain the way they experience different kinds of attraction.

The split-attraction model recognizes that sexual, romantic, and other attractions are not intrinsically connected, and that they can work independently of each other. So a person can be asexual (experiencing no or little sexual attraction) but be alloromantic (experiencing romantic attraction). Or a person can be allosexual (experiencing sexual attraction) but be aromantic (experiencing little or no romantic attraction).

The model also allows for splits in the directionality of different attractions. So a person can be asexual and identify as homoromantic (experiencing romantic attraction for people of the same gender) or be aromantic and pansexual (experiencing sexual attraction for people without regard to gender). The split-attraction model also allows for both to have directionalities: A person could be bisexual (experiencing sexual attraction for two or more genders) and heteroromantic (experiencing romantic attraction for someone of a different gender).

While the split-attraction model primarily looks at two attractions—sexual and romantic—it can be used to describe relationships to the other attractions as well. And although the model is most commonly used by a-spec individuals—individuals on either or both of the asexual and aromantic spectrums—it can be used by other sexual orientations as a tool to more completely communicate a person's experience of attraction.

When people find the split-attraction model useful, they are often responding to the way it articulates an individual's unique experience of attraction: where it occurs, where it doesn't, and in what direction any particular attraction is moving.

Do asexual people have sex?

If I had a dollar for every time someone asked me this question since coming out as asexual, I'd have an obscene amount of dollars.

In short, the answer is yes. Asexual people can and do have sex.

Remember that stereotype we talked about earlier, of the asexual blank slate? That stereotype comes into play here. It's assumed that because asexual people don't experience sexual attraction, they will also completely reject physical intimacy of all kinds, including sex.

But that's not how asexuality works. Asexuality is only about an individual's experience of sexual attraction. It doesn't speak to one's relationship to sexual behavior.

There are lots of reasons beyond sexual attraction that a person would engage in sexual behavior. People have sex to experience closeness with their partners. They have sex to procreate and raise children. They have sex to express other attractions they may feel for a partner. They have sex simply because it feels good, and they enjoy the physical sensations.

You can have sex without experiencing sexual attraction. So asexual people can have sex.

Is celibacy or abstinence the same as asexuality?

There are people who, for reasons of their own, choose not to engage in sexual activity.

When a person decides not to engage in any sexual activity, we call it abstinence. It's a decision one makes about their sexual behaviors, and abstinence can last for as little or as long as a person wants it to last.

Celibacy is also a choice an individual makes not to engage in sexual activity; however, celibacy suggests a much longer-term commitment to abstaining from sexual activity. Celibacy also, in some contexts, includes a decision to forgo marriage as well. It's a more serious, permanent commitment to abstaining. It's why you often hear it referred to as a "vow of celibacy."

Abstinence and celibacy mean you're not having sex. But neither of them mean you're asexual.

Abstinence and celibacy represent choices people make about their behaviors surrounding sex. Two words are important here: choices and behaviors.

In the vast majority of cases, people choose abstinence and

celibacy. There are situations in which people are coerced or forced into these behaviors, but those situations aren't the norm. Asexuality isn't a choice. Asexual people don't choose to be asexual. It's not a switch we can turn on and off as we wish. So in this way, abstinence and celibacy aren't asexuality.

Abstinence and celibacy also focus on sexual *behaviors*. They're about what people choose to do with their bodies. Asexuality isn't defined by behavior. Asexuality isn't about what we do. Asexuality is about how we experience attraction. It's about what we feel, what we experience. Through this lens, as well, abstinence and celibacy aren't asexuality.

An asexual person can choose to abstain from sex. An asexual person can also choose to be celibate. But those choices and behaviors are not what make that person asexual. And choosing abstinence or celibacy won't make an allosexual person suddenly asexual.

What makes a person asexual is that they do not experience or rarely experience sexual attraction.

What if I'm not sure what attractions I'm feeling? How do I know who I am?

If there's one thing that's defined my experience discovering, processing, and understanding my asexuality, it's the feeling of uncertainty. I'm almost four years into my own journey, and there are still things that confuse me, things that surprise me, things that knock me over and punch me in the gut with their unexpectedness. I feel similarly about other aspects of my queerness, even with parts of my queerness that have been in my life for decades. I'm still learning things about my romantic orientation. I'm still learning things about my gender. The complicated parts of me, the things that don't line up with the dominant culture's expectations, are always revealing new things about themselves.

Uncertainty is maybe the only thing that's been consistent

throughout these processes. Being unsure is kind of the name of the game.

In order to survive this journey of self-discovery, you have to give yourself permission to not know. There's no harm in not knowing. There's no failure in not knowing. It's perfectly human to live in your body and experience what you're experiencing without fully understanding it.

The *curiosity* is what counts. What counts is you acknowledging that you feel something different from the people around you. What counts is that you're searching for new words and new ideas to explain what you feel instead of shoving those feelings away and just conforming to the rest of the world.

What counts is your question, even if you don't have an answer.

Chapter 3
WHAT KIND OF ASEXUAL AM I?

I discovered asexuality while scrolling through Tumblr. I was 42 years old.

My husband is 14 years younger than me, and I learned about Tumblr through him.

"It's a good time-waster," he said.

"But, it's like...where the *kids* are," I said.

"A lot of people use Tumblr, and it's not just kids," he said, rolling his eyes at me. "You'll find the stuff you dig, and if you curate the accounts you follow the right way, it'll just be a *stream* of stuff you dig, whenever you want. It's totally your jam. Try it."

Horror stuff? Check. Art stuff? Check. Queer stuff? Check. The occasional chubby hairy guy to gawk at? Check. Check. Check.

It was a good time-waster, and as someone in love with shiny new things and prone to hyperfixations, Tumblr became a constant digital companion.

It was in all that scrolling that I started to see posts about asexuality. I was aware of asexuality, and I thought I had a basic understanding of what it was. I knew it had something to do with not wanting to have sex, or maybe it was about not having sex. Or something like that. I know it was in that ballpark, but I didn't know *exactly* what it was.

(I'd soon find out I didn't know *anything* about asexuality. I knew *nothing*. I was exactly the kind of person who needed this book.)

The asexuality posts I found on Tumblr were a startling education. They were the first place I saw asexuality properly defined and the first place I learned that my assumed definition was completely wrong. This was also my first encounter with the spectrum of asexuality (demisexual! gray-asexual! microlabels!) and the first time I'd encountered people talking about what asexuality felt like, how they came to know they were ace, and how they lived as ace in the world.

I felt two things.

The first was unsurprising: I felt bad. I felt bad that, as an out queer man for over two decades, I didn't know this stuff already. I should know about my queer family. Here was a whole world of queer lives that I'd just made assumptions about—assumptions that were wrong and, in some cases, downright damaging. I chose lazy assumption over constructive curiosity, and my queer family deserved better than that.

But I also felt something entirely unexpected: I felt *seen*. I saw myself in these posts. My reluctance and discomfort with the act of sex. A disinterest in sex I felt was wholly unlike my queer male peers. A nagging feeling of difference, of being an Other among Others, that had always followed me around sex and intimacy. Here was a language describing 20 years of my experience. My life, which I'd always assumed was just a broken form of "normal," had a name.

I was *asexual*.

Finding a name for my experience changed my life. It reconfigured how I saw myself and how I related to the world and the people around me. The more I dug into the resources on asexuality and the more I learned about the many labels within the ace spectrum, the more I understood myself. It was liberating.

As ace folks, we go through much of our lives searching for the language to describe what we feel. We don't see our experiences reflected in the world. We don't see them depicted in the media we encounter and consume. And we don't recognize them in the people we surround ourselves with. We feel like these little islands of experience, isolated, alone in what we feel.

So when we discover the language of asexuality, it's like turning on a light in a darkened room. Finding words that describe the very things we've experienced—things we thought were either unique to us or proof that we were some broken versions of "normal people"—reframes the way we look at our experiences and transforms the way we think about ourselves.

In this chapter, we're going to explore the language of asexuality—the labels, large and small, that distinguish different experiences within the asexual spectrum. Recognizing you're asexual is the first step on this identity journey. Exploring the language of asexuality and finding the right words to describe how you experience asexuality is the next step.

Labels are tools, not tests

Before we dive into the deep end with the language of asexuality, I want to talk about what labels do and what they don't.

Identity labels have two main functions. Labels exist to help you articulate your particular experience to yourself and to others. And labels exist to help you find community with other people who share your particular experience.

That's it. That's the ballgame.

Labels don't create rigid definitions that you must either fit completely or be excluded from. Labels don't establish complicated checklists that you must measure yourself up against in order to use them. Labels don't create walls that divide us into "us" and "them." Labels don't construct measures of purity or validity that determine who's worthy and who's not.

Labels are tools, not tests.

Let's hear that one more time: Labels are tools, not tests.

Labels exist to help you. So as you move through this chapter and start to compare your own experience against the experiences described by the language of asexuality, don't worry if nothing is the perfect fit. Don't worry if multiple labels are the perfect fit. Don't worry if everything you encounter is both right and wrong and everything in between.

Labels are tools you can use to build your asexual identity. They work for you, not the other way around.

The asexual spectrum

As we discussed in Chapter 1, asexuality is not a singular or monolithic experience. It's a spectrum of experience, containing many different modes and variations of being asexual.

In the broadest sense and at the highest level, asexual is a term that encompasses the entirety of that spectrum. Anyone who identifies among the people who do not experience or rarely experience sexual attraction can call themselves asexual, with many of us using the shortened form: ace.

You may also encounter the label a-spec, which is another high-level term that includes anyone on the asexual and aromantic spectrum. A person doesn't have to be on both spectrums to use a-spec. The term can apply to those who belong to one or both spectrums.

This language is useful when speaking about the community as a whole or when referring to the broad experience of asexuality. However, it's not wise to assume that every person in the community will use these words as self-identifiers. For some, this high-level label is insufficient or not specific to their experience. So, be mindful of the language people use to describe themselves, and be open to correction if someone generally identifies by a more specific label.

The asexual spectrum: the umbrella labels

Under the broad and high-level labels of asexual/a-spec that describe the spectrum, there are a handful of more specific labels that describe more specific experiences that individuals may have with sexual attraction.

For our purposes, let's call them the umbrella labels.

The umbrella labels give some shape to the asexuality spectrum, broadly defining some of the spaces between those on the spectrum who never experience sexual attraction and those on the spectrum who sometimes do. These are the labels that appear most frequently in conversations about asexuality, and a significant number of ace individuals use one of these labels as a self-identifier.

As with the labels asexual and a-spec, the umbrella labels are also not universal. For some on the asexual spectrum, even these labels lack the specificity they're looking for. Be mindful of what language a person uses to self-identify, and respect those choices.

What follows are the umbrella labels.

Asexual

Asexual can be used in two contexts on the spectrum. As we discussed, it's used as the overarching term for members of the community. But it is also used by people on the asexual spectrum who do not experience sexual attraction.

While the two definitions might seem interchangeable, "asexual" in the latter context describes a more specific experience on the asexual spectrum. Ace individuals who use "asexual" as their self-identifier have not, as a rule, experienced sexual attraction.

It's important to remember that "not experiencing sexual attraction" is how most people think of all asexuals.

Graysexual

Graysexual (or gray-asexual) is used by people on the asexual spectrum that sometimes experience or rarely experience sexual attraction. It's also a word used by folks on the spectrum who only ever experience sexual attraction at a very low intensity. It can also be used by individuals who feel strong connection to the asexual experience but may not feel completely described by that label.

Like asexual, graysexual can either be used as a specific identity label or it can be used more broadly to describe the group of labels that describe those who sometimes experience or rarely experience sexual attraction. Some graysexual folks will use a shortened form: gray-ace.

Demisexual
Demisexual is used by people on the asexual spectrum who only experience sexual attraction when they develop an emotional bond with someone. Without an emotional bond, they either do not experience sexual attraction or only experience it very rarely.

Sometimes the bond formed needs to be strong and intense. Sometimes, demisexual folks only require a soft emotional bond. But in all cases, that emotional bond is the important distinction. And it's important to note that an emotional bond doesn't *guarantee* a demisexual person will feel sexual attraction. It makes it possible, not a certainty.

Sometimes, demisexuality is considered part of the graysexual umbrella. Sometimes, it's simply considered a category on its own. Both are acceptable.

Aceflux
Aceflux is used by people on the asexual spectrum who experience fluctuation in their sexual orientation but stay mainly on the asexual spectrum. Aceflux individuals may sometimes feel allosexual and sometimes feel asexual. Aceflux individuals may also just experience fluctuation across the asexual spectrum, feeling demisexual sometimes and asexual other times.

What's important here is the fluctuation.

These identity labels for the asexual spectrum aren't comprehensive. There are other broad labels that are newly created or only minimally used by ace folks, and there are a host of microlabels we'll discuss in a moment. But these identities give you a general picture of who falls under the asexual umbrella.

These labels can be used in conjunction with other labels, or they can be used on their own. It's up to you. Remember, labels are tools. Use them accordingly.

Microlabels

For a lot of us, the big umbrella terms are adequate: asexual, graysexual, demisexual, aceflux. But some of us need or seek out something more. We seek out words that more specifically describe our unique relationship to sex and sexual attraction.

That's where microlabels come in.

Microlabels are the identity labels that fall under the umbrella of the larger identity labels, and they describe a specific, particular experience under that umbrella label. Microlabels don't typically stand on their own. If you identify as one of the microlabels, it often implies that one of the umbrella labels also applies. But there's no rule on how microlabels are used; they can be used on their own to describe one's identity. They can also be used in conjunction with other labels to describe one's identity.

The "micro" of microlabel doesn't suggest anything about the prevalence of the identity, how well it's known in various communities, or its perceived importance compared to other identities. It just means that this identity props up or clarifies a broader identity term. Microlabels make someone's identity clearer, more specific, more precise.

Why do we even need microlabels?

"Well, if there are already words to describe your identity, why do you need these other, weirder ones?"

This question gets leveled at people who use microlabels all the time. For people who feel adequately defined by the umbrella labels, using these more niche, unknown microlabels can seem confusing and unnecessary. But microlabels serve several important functions for the people who use them.

First, microlabels help people find the exact language for their experience. Human sexuality is a complicated thing. So much goes into defining our specific experience of sex and sexual attraction: our innate attractions, the specific workings of our libido, the experiences we have with relationships, the messages we receive from our families and friends about sex, the ways we relate to and are influenced by cultural messages about sex. We can be shaped by so many forces, and we can respond to those forces in so many different ways, that sometimes our experience of the world and ourselves cannot be adequately described by a label as broad as "asexual" or "demisexual." Microlabels step into this space, and they give us more options—more precise options—for describing who we are and what we feel and experience.

Microlabels are also community builders. The asexual spectrum is a broad one. There's no monolithic way to be ace. There are lots of different ways to be asexual. And while that diversity is one of the things that make the ace spectrum so great, it can also make it harder for some ace folks to find others who experience asexuality the way they do. That can feel isolating, othering.

Imagine the feeling of going through your life feeling completely out of step with the world, then finally discovering a community that speaks your language, only to find, once you're in the community, that you still feel out of step. Microlabels make that easier. Because they're describing specific relationships to sex and sexual attraction, when you find others who use the same microlabels, you're finding your people. And in sexual minorities like the asexual community, finding your people is important.

Some microlabels

Here are just some of the microlabels that fall under the asexual spectrum.

Aegosexual

Aegosexual is a microlabel that describes people who experience a disconnect between themselves and the subjects of sexual desire. In more simple terms, aegosexuals experience comfort with the idea of sex, but they experience a discomfort or aversion to actually participating in it.

Aegosexuals might feel comfortable talking about sex, engaging with sexual media and content (like erotic stories or pornography), or fantasizing about sexual encounters. But they won't necessarily feel comfortable acting on any of those things.

You might see aegosexuality sometimes referred to as "autochorissexuality." This was the original microlabel for this experience. But the expert who coined the phrase considered it a paraphilia (a condition of abnormal sexual desires). So, another term was coined, one that didn't consider the experience to be abnormal or dangerous.

Lithosexual

Lithosexual is a microlabel that describes people who may experience sexual attraction but do not want it reciprocated. Lithosexual individuals also sometimes lose sexual attraction or sexual feelings if they learn those feelings are reciprocated.

Akoisexual is another term used to describe the same experience.

Fictosexual

Fictosexual is a microlabel that describes people who only experience sexual attraction toward specific fictional characters or types of fictional characters. Fictosexuals do not, however, experience sexual attraction to people in the non-fictional world.

Sometimes, fictosexuals are attracted to certain types of characters (like anime characters, video game characters, or supernatural characters).

Apothisexual

Apothisexual is a microlabel that describes asexual people who are repulsed by the idea of sex. For some apothisexuals, this repulsion is total. They are repulsed by the idea of them having sex and by the general idea of sex. For some apothisexuals, that repulsion is only about having sex themselves.

"Sex-repulsed," a term we'll come across shortly, is another bit of language that can be used by apothisexuals.

Cupiosexual

Cupiosexual is a microlabel that describes asexual people who desire a sexual relationship. Cupiosexuals don't experience sexual attraction or only do in rare situations, but they do, on the whole, seek out and desire sexual relationships.

"Sex-favorable," another term we'll encounter shortly, can be useful to folks who are cupiosexual.

Placiosexual

Placiosexual is a microlabel on the asexual spectrum that describes someone who is willing to or enjoys performing sexual acts on a partner but has strong negative feelings, even repulsion, about having sexual acts performed on them.

A term for the opposite of this—being willing or enjoying having sexual acts performed on you but feeling repulsed about performing sexual acts on others—exists: iamvanosexual.

Fraysexual

Fraysexual describes someone who only experiences sexual attraction for someone they have no deep connection with. As bonds develop, fraysexuals no longer experience sexual attraction, although they may continue to pursue sexual relationships.

Some think of fraysexuality as the inverse experience of demisexuality.

Caedsexual

Caedsexuals are individuals who did experience sexual attraction at one point but feel that attraction was stripped away or "cut out" by some kind of past trauma.

Caedsexual should only be used by those who have survived trauma or experience PTSD. Its existence is very specifically tied to those communities, so respecting that boundary when using this microlabel or adopting it for yourself is important.

Reciprosexual

Reciprosexual is a microlabel on the asexual spectrum that describes individuals who do not experience sexual attraction until they know a person is sexually attracted to them.

This is not to be confused with someone who only decides to pursue sexual activity until they know someone is into them. That's behavior, not orientation. Reciprosexuals don't experience any sexual attraction unless someone has clearly expressed that they are sexually attracted to them.

Quoisexual

Quoisexual is a label that describes a set of similar, overlapping experiences and feelings about sexual attraction. Quoisexual folks can be unsure whether or not they experience sexual attraction or be unsure about what constitutes sexual attraction. Quoisexual folks may not understand the idea of sexual attraction or feel they have no relation to sexual attraction at all. Quoisexual folks may also simply not be able to distinguish, within themselves, the difference between sexual attraction and other kinds of attraction.

For individuals who experience considerable difficulty parsing out the specifics of their own relationship to attraction and intimacy, quoisexual is a label that can provide a much-needed sense of self and community.

These aren't the only microlabels that exist. There are many others, and new microlabels are created all the time. These just provide a window into the world of microlabels.

Do I need to find a microlabel for myself?

Finding a microlabel that fits your experience isn't a necessity. If one of the umbrella identities fits you and feels right as a description of your experience, then you're perfectly fine sticking with that.

But if you feel like those words don't quite nail it, if you feel that the umbrella terms tell only half of your story, then maybe a microlabel is right for you. Remember, labels are tools. They are designed to help you communicate your experience and help you find community. Use the words that achieve those goals. Don't bother with the ones that don't.

The language of physical intimacy

Beyond the need for a language that describes the spectrum of our relationships to sexual attraction, asexual folks have a need for a language that describes their relationship to sexual activity and physical intimacy. (Remember, those two things operate independently.)

So the language of asexuality includes a set of labels that describe different degrees of comfort with physical intimacy and different degrees of willingness to engage in sexual activity. This language helps to further clarify the fullness of our identities, and the wholeness of how we interact with the world and other people.

Sex-favorable

Sex-favorable folks are asexual and a-spec individuals who enjoy the act of sex or the idea of sex. Sex-favorable folks don't experience or rarely experience sexual attraction, but they find pleasure in the act of sex for other reasons: they just enjoy it physically, they use it to express another kind of attraction they feel toward someone (romantic attraction, for example), or they enjoy pleasing a partner through sexual activity. Sex-favorable folks can have a little sex or a lot of it. But being sex-favorable doesn't mean someone's down for anything and everything. Just like allosexual folks, sex-favorable ace folks can have specific boundaries around certain kinds of sexual activity.

Sex-neutral

Sex-neutral folks are asexual or a-spec folks who do not experience strong feelings in either direction about sexual activity. There are no strong negative feelings about it, but there aren't strong positive feelings about it either. Sex-neutral folks can feel this way about the idea of personally engaging in sexual activity and about the idea of sex in general. Some sex-neutral folks choose not to have sex. Some do, for reasons like connecting with their partner or having children. What's important for sex-neutral folks is having no strong pull in either direction in regard to sexual activity.

Sex-averse

Sex-averse folks are asexual or a-spec individuals who experience some negative feelings toward sex. But these negative feelings are primarily focused on the idea of them personally engaging in sexual activity. There can be a comfort level in the idea of sex, in the idea of other people having sex. Sex-averse folks may be comfortable talking or joking about sex. They're just not comfortable having it, and they may decide not to make sex a part of their lives or relationships.

Sex-repulsed

Sex-repulsed folks are asexual and a-spec folks who experience strong negative feelings toward sex. This can include not just the thought of having sex but the idea of sex in general. Sex-repulsed folks not only may experience serious discomfort around the idea of having sex, but they also might experience some discomfort around talking about sex, joking about sex, or seeing sexual content in movies, TV shows, or books. For some sex-repulsed folks, this feeling can be so strong that it becomes physical. They can experience real physical disgust, like cringing, shaking, or nausea.

This language is often used in tandem with other labels in the language of asexuality. For example, I alternate between sex-neutral and sex-favorable asexual. And as with all of the language of asexuality, these are not hard and fast labels with rigid boundaries. There is flexibility within these labels. As your relationship to sexual activity changes, the label you use can change.

These labels are also not the exclusive territory of a-spec folks. Even though we use these labels more, allosexual folks who also experience varying degrees of comfort and willingness around sexual activity can use these labels to clarify their own identities.

Why do labels feel so intimidating?

Okay. Let's take a deep breath here.

It's very easy to feel intimidated by the abundance of labels that make up the language of asexuality. In just a few pages, we've covered a complex web of interlocking labels that sometimes work together and sometimes work independently and that attempt to define an almost impossibly wide array of experiences around sexual attraction and activity.

If that feels intimidating, that's okay. In many ways, it is. This language describes experiences that rarely ever get spoken about, rarely ever get represented in any mainstream media, and rarely ever receive validation. You can't expect to immediately know how to relate to this language if it and the experiences it describes are mostly new to you. It's like traveling to France without speaking French and expecting to be fluent on day one.

Part of that intimidation and part of the anxiety many of us feel around labels stems from what we think labels do.

Many of us think labels describe who we *are*. We believe they describe a fundamental state of being we inhabit, a fixed, immovable truth about us. We believe that when we choose a label, we are choosing something we must fully embody with all of our being, now and forever. Because the label is what we *are*.

And in some ways, that's true. Our identities do feel deeply rooted, and they do feel like immutable truths. But that's a lot of pressure for a handful of words to shoulder, particularly when the reality of identity is of an ongoing process, not a singular destination. This view of labels also locks us into a life without evolution, growth, and change. This view assumes that once we find a label, we stop learning new things about ourselves and the world. We stop becoming.

So to alleviate that pressure, we should not think of labels so much as what we *are*, but we should think of them as descriptors of what we *experience*. Experience isn't fixed and immutable. Experience isn't something we have to embody with all of our being. Experience is a moment we pass through, a little bit of friction between us and the world, that teaches us one part of who we are and who we might be.

It's much less intimidating to think of labels as describing what's happening to us right now, as opposed to who we are forever.

Can you use more than one label on the asexual spectrum?

Absolutely.

The language of asexuality is not a scarcity culture. There isn't "only so much to go around," and you aren't expected to winnow your options down to the one label that encompasses all that you are, choose it, and live desperately by that one label for the rest of your life.

The language of asexuality is abundant and incredibly flexible. The words we use to describe asexuality accomplish a lot of things. Some of the words describe broad experiences. Some of the words describe very specific experiences with sex and attraction. And in many cases, the broad words and the specific words overlap, describe similar things, and operate together to define experience as opposed to operating independently.

So, yes. You can have more than one identity on the asexual spectrum. You can describe who you are using multiple labels. You can create a combination of labels that articulate your full experience.

The language of asexuality exists to work for you. Not the other way around. If multiple words speak to your experience, then use them. If one word speaks to your experience, use it.

What matters is that the words you use are serving you. That's their job. That's their function.

I can't find a label that fits me exactly. Is something wrong with me?

Language is often imprecise, and that's never more true than for identity labels.

Identity labels, even microlabels, are designed to describe ranges of experience. They aren't built to capture specificity and nuance. They're built to draw somewhat heavy-handed lines around general groupings of experiences. So more often than not, even with the labels that drill down on finer sub-experiences, what you experience as an individual won't be fully contained by any one label.

And that makes sense, right? You're a complicated human being living a nuanced life shaped by a lot of internal and external forces. Language, no matter how thoughtful or considered, will fall short of encompassing it.

Somehow, though, we internalize a belief that the opposite should be true. We believe that we should look into language and find a mirror of who we are. When we don't find that mirror, we don't assume there's something wrong with the words. We assume there's something wrong with us.

Identity language isn't a custom-made suit, tailored to fit us in every detail. Identity language is a one-size-fits-all baseball cap. A lot of folks can wear it. It doesn't fit exactly, but it's close enough. And it serves its function when you're wearing it.

If you can't find the words that speak precisely of your experience, find the words that get close to it.

Don't forget: Change is a constant

When you start feeling overwhelmed by the complexity and nuance of identity language, just remember: You're a person first, label later.

We're human beings. We specialize in change. We grow. We learn. We reassess. We reconsider. We toss out old ideas. We adopt new ones. We are always in a process of evolving who we are. It's just what we're built to do.

Why should our labels be different? Why shouldn't they grow and learn and change with us? Why shouldn't we toss out old ones and adopt new ones? Why shouldn't they be as fluid and evolving as we are?

At the end of the day, they're just words. Who you are and what you experience, whether attached to the words or not, is always the more important thing.

Chapter 4
BUT AM I *REALLY* ASEXUAL?

"**Y**ou know you're asexual, right?" It was the first time I'd said those words out loud.

I'd been thinking those words for weeks, often spurred by an obsessive reading and re-reading of this one particular Tumblr post about asexuality that I'd saved on an open browser tab. It was one of those "you know you're asexual if..." posts, with a considerable string of replies. I could have written the post myself. I related to everything on the list and most of the replies.

You're not sure if you ever experienced sexual attraction.

You've felt pressured to have sex because it's what you're "supposed to do."

You don't understand why people complain about not having sex.

You've made up a crush to fit in with your peers.

Your peers' obsession with sex makes you uncomfortable.

And on and on and on. I ticked all the boxes, or at least was pretty close.

That's me, I'd tell myself every time I read it. *That's what I feel. What I've felt forever. Maybe I'm asexual. Maybe that's the thing.*

I brooded about it for weeks, but I never said the words out loud. I was afraid of that. There's an additional layer of power to speaking that sort of thing out loud, that leap from thought to action. If you give it a name, you have to do something with it.

That morning, standing in front of the bathroom mirror, about to brush my teeth, I considered the me who'd been brooding for weeks. I always thought he was broken, somehow. Awkward and just really bad at sex and intimacy stuff. He was a sad, insecure guy who had felt out of sync with himself and the world for years, this brooding me, the me staring back in the mirror.

Maybe the thing I'd been thinking was something he needed to hear.

"You know you're asexual, right?"

I guess I expected it to be an incantation. I believed if I spoke it, then suddenly I'd fully *be* it, and the True Asexual Cody would appear in a swirl of gray, purple, black, and white. He'd be confident and complete, and he'd leave the bathroom and go into the world some kind of asexual superhero.

Instead, I was just staring at myself with a toothbrush in my hand wondering what to do next.

Finding asexuality was a relief for me. Finally, here was a word for all the confusing and difficult feelings I'd felt. But finding the language didn't change my reality. Sure, I knew what to call it. But I didn't know how to *live* it. I still had to figure out how asexuality and I fit together, and how to clear out the dusty baggage of my old reality to make space for this new one.

Finding a language for who we are is only half the journey. Owning that language, taking those words as fact, and truly living them is the other half, the harder half. In this chapter, we'll go beyond the language of asexuality and explore the doubts, fears, and insecurities we feel as we try on the language and the identity. We'll learn some strategies to overcome those fears and doubts, and we'll learn why this process is so difficult in the first place.

Why is figuring this out so hard?

When you look at the world, you rarely see asexual people.

Think about the media we consume: television, movies, books, music, theater, all forms of media across all platforms. You don't see a lot of ace lives or ace relationships. Sure, you see us every now and then. There's Jughead in the *Archie* comics. There's that one scene in *Sex Education* on Netflix that gets sent to anyone and everyone who comes out as ace. There are some good ace books (Alice Oseman's *Loveless* and T. J. Klune's *How to Be a Normal Person*), but they don't often get the same level of attention as books centering non-ace characters do.

Now, think about the visible role models around us. We rarely see an openly asexual celebrity. There are no big-name Hollywood actors or musicians who are visibly ace. We have no famous ace politicians or elected officials. How many of us have had openly ace teachers or mentors? How many of us even know another openly ace person in real life?

Ace representation, in media and in the real world, exists, but it's often hard to find. And when you stack it up next to the representation available for allosexual identities, ace representation is just a drop in the ocean. We're "blink and you miss us."

And this makes figuring out your asexuality a lot harder.

One of the ways we understand who we are in the world is by finding reflections of ourselves in it. We go through our lives collecting feelings and experiences, then we go looking for the people or representations in the world that mirror those feelings and experiences. We search for people and representations that give us a language for who we are and what's happening to us. When we find it, we go, "That's me! That's what I am!" And we understand who we are.

With so little representation in the world, ace folks have lifetimes of feelings and experiences, but we look out into a world where nothing mirrors what we feel. No one speaks our language. Our experiences and feelings don't match up to anything visible to us. And when all we see are things not matching up, we begin to believe there's something wrong with us. Instead of finding a language for who we are, we find a language for feeling shame in who we are.

Another problem is sex.

On the one hand, we treat sex as something ultimately desirable and supremely valuable. Sex is everywhere. It's a plot point in practically every movie or TV show we consume. It's at the heart of a lot of our most popular music. Sex is used to sell us everything from cars to crop tops to coffee. It's a ubiquitous cultural message, an idealized and homogenized vision of sex and sexuality that's at once a universal expectation and an unattainable standard.

At the same time, we want to pretend sex doesn't exist. We want sex to stay behind closed doors and in whispered conversations. We socially punish those who fully embrace and are proud of their sexuality. We moralize and demonize anyone who fully lives in and enjoys their body, particularly when they use their bodies in ways that disrupt or subvert cultural expectations. Our culture treats the true variety and diversity of sex as something dangerous and taboo. Sure, we want sex, but we want it to stay in a culturally controlled box, neatly organized into clear-cut roles and rules, no gray areas, no fuzzy definitions.

But sex is nothing like that. Sex is all gray areas, all fuzzy definitions.

So, we're obsessed with sex, but not as sex really is. We consider sex shameful, but not if it's useful to reinforce social hierarchies or to further the goals of capitalism. These two opposing ideas cause a great deal of cultural friction, so much so that we don't have a good language for talking about sex in general, much less sexual identities specifically. We only "kinda sorta" talk about sex. Which does no one any good.

This makes things even harder for ace folks. Not only are we trying to understand something with a "kinda sorta" language, but we're trying to understand it from the outside. We're *not* experiencing something everyone else is and is taking for granted, so it's a double "kinda sorta." And it makes understanding any sexuality outside of the dominant cultural norm incredibly difficult.

It's okay if you're confused about whether or not you're asexual. It's kind of a miracle that anyone ever stops being confused. The cultural cards are stacked against us.

Forget the definitions; focus on what you *experience*

How do we begin to counter this confusion? We can begin by
rethinking our relationship to the language of asexuality.

Definitions are comforting. They take an idea, no matter how big,
and give it a shape. Definitions wrestle all the unknown things in the
world and help us know them. With a definition, we know what is and
what is not, and where the line between those two things resides. That
makes people feel safe, in control.

The problem is definitions are limited. Because all of human
experience resists definition. Life is most beautiful when it's messy and
unpredictable, when it's big, unwieldy, and full of variety. Life wants to
get rid of all the lines, all the boxes. It just wants to be.

So when we focus on the definitions, like the definitions of
asexuality, and think that our experience is only valid if it lines up, letter
by letter, word by word, with the definitions, we're setting ourselves up
for a very confusing time.

Instead of focusing on definitions, we should focus on our
experience. We should focus on what we feel.

What do you feel when you think of asexuality? What do you feel
when you connect asexuality with yourself? What do you feel when
you say, out loud, "I am ace?"

What have you felt when it comes to attraction? If you've had
sexual experiences, what did you feel when they were happening?
When you think about sex, what feelings come up for you? When you
think about not having sex, what feelings come up then?

You'll probably feel a lot of different things, some of them
contradictory, but those feelings will tell you a lot. Those feelings
have nothing to do with cultural norms and expectations. They aren't
connected to what your parents want for you and what your friends
expect of you. You're not measuring these feelings against anyone or
anything else. You're just listening to what you have to say about your
own experience. What you have to say about you.

When you strip all of that other stuff away, and you're telling yourself, "Asexuality feels right," it doesn't matter what the definitions are or if you fit them word for word.

The language of asexuality, all of the definitions and all of the identity labels, isn't there as a test. It's there as a tool to help you explain yourself to yourself and to explain yourself to the world. The definitions and labels are tools to help you find community.

That's all.

When you're not sure what you're feeling, be sure of what you're not

"But I don't know what I'm experiencing! I don't know what I'm feeling!"

I've been there. We all have.

Because there are so many ways to be ace, locating yourself among the infinite options offered by the asexuality spectrum can be incredibly difficult. Sometimes the distinctions aren't clear. Sometimes the language leaves too much room for interpretation. Sometimes we can find bits and pieces of our individual experience scattered across several different labels or definitions. Sometimes our individual experience, when measured up against the language of asexuality, can feel contradictory and confusing.

We can be experiencing and feeling entire worlds of things but have no idea how to think or talk about it.

Let's turn to a very famous asexual headcanon giant, the great Sherlock Holmes, as written by the legendary Sir Arthur Conan Doyle, for some advice here.

"How often have I said to you that when you have eliminated the impossible, whatever remains, *however improbable*, must be the truth?"

He wasn't talking about asexuality, but he could have been. While the basic definition of asexuality is simple, the implications of that definition open up a world of complicated asides and digressions. Most ace folks have had countless conversations like this:

"Yeah, so I'm asexual."

"What's that mean?"

"Asexuals don't experience sexual attraction."

"So they don't have sex."

"No. That's behavior. That's separate. Asexuality is only talking about sexual attraction."

"Well, what's sexual attraction?"

"It's being attracted to someone and having that attraction make you want to have sex with them."

"So, like having sex and falling in love and all of that?"

"No. Love is about romantic attraction. That's different."

"Okay. So asexuals just don't experience sexual attraction at all?"

"No. Well, *some* do. Demisexuals and graysexuals do experience sexual attraction sometimes. As can aceflux folks. But only under specific circumstances."

"Oh. Okay. So the key thing is not wanting to have sex sometimes."

"Well, not exactly. That's behavior, remember. You can want to have sex sometimes. There are sex-favorable ace folks."

"So it's just about not experiencing attraction—"

"*Sexual* attraction. You can experience other kinds of attraction. Aesthetic. Romantic. Emotional. Sensual."

"Okay, okay... I. Okay."

So when the process of lining ourselves up against the language of asexuality becomes challenging, it's good to stop, take a break, and shift gears.

Sometimes the best course of action is just figuring out what's *not* true. What's *not* there.

I came out as asexual when I was 42. But way before then—for over two decades—I knew I was different. I knew there were things about sex that I just didn't feel, things I didn't experience or understand. My friends were relating to sex one way, and I was not there with them. I didn't understand what I was. But I could clearly see what I was not.

It's like when there's a really popular show on television. Like *Game of Thrones*. And everyone's watching it. Everyone's tweeting about it and talking about it at work. Every episode: BAM! No matter where you turn, someone's talking about dragons or sharing a meme about "hold the door." But you don't watch *Game of Thrones*. You've never seen *Game of Thrones*. All you know about *Game of Thrones* is what everyone else is saying about it.

That's how I felt about sex. Everyone was talking about it and tweeting about it and sharing memes about it, and I could tell the memes were funny, but *I didn't know why*. In a world of *Game of Thrones*, I was watching *RuPaul's Drag Race*.

I knew what *wasn't* there. And that guided me with more clarity and more confidence toward knowing myself as an asexual person than any of the hours I spent trying to figure out what I *was* feeling.

If you eliminate the things that are impossible or the things that simply *aren't*, and you're left with asexuality—even if you don't exactly fit every definition, word for word, or if you still have questions and are a little unsure—asexuality, however improbable, just might be the truth.

But how do I know it's asexuality and not something else?

There's a whole flock of "what ifs" that circle overhead when we're questioning whether or not we're ace.

What if I just have a hormone imbalance? What if I just have a naturally low libido? What if I'm just anxious about being intimate with someone? What if it's just the way my parents raised me? What if it's unresolved trauma from my past? What if I'm just confusing some other thing for asexuality?

These "what ifs" are persistent, and they're all, in some ways, legitimate questions to ask ourselves. We should be thorough in our exploration of our identity, looking at all the possibilities and considering them fairly.

But many of us spend a long time—sometimes years—focusing exclusively on these alternate possibilities, wrestling with them and agonizing over them, keeping ourselves from fully embracing ourselves as anything at all. We sometimes use these alternate explanations as ways to shield us from the possible reality of our asexuality, as though asexuality can only be the truth if it's the last option.

It's healthy to consider the "what ifs." It's not healthy to fixate on them. When we use these "what ifs" as shields against asexuality, when we reach for alternate answers because we're afraid the answer is asexuality, we're limiting our ability to know ourselves fully. We're forcing a narrative instead of simply letting our story unfold.

And here's a hard truth: Maybe it's some of those things *and* asexuality. Maybe some of the "what ifs" have informed or colored your sexual orientation. Maybe the answer to your identity journey is "and" instead of "or." Lots of things shape our overall experience: our innate feelings, our specific physical realities, how our brains work, our experiences in the world, our experiences in relationships with other people. A complex combination of these disparate forces doesn't have to be explained by one thing alone. Our asexuality doesn't have to, either.

So ponder the "what ifs." But ponder all of them. Give yourself the best shot to truly understand yourself, whatever that truth may be.

I think I'm asexual, but am I too young to know that?

Young people, particularly young queer people, hear this often. "You're too young to know you're gay." "You're too young to know you're transgender." "You're too young to know you're asexual."

No one, however, questions that young straight people truly know they're straight. No one questions that young cisgender people know they're cisgender. Everyone is assumed to be allosexual, so no adult will bat an eye when a young person says they're sexually attracted to someone.

Only queerness, in whatever form it takes, is considered strictly an adult experience.

Why?

By treating queerness as something that only happens to adults (and, further, is only something that happens to "broken" or "bad" adults), it creates permission to remove anything and everything queer from the world of young people. If queerness is "adults only," then there's justification to remove any books about queerness, movies about queerness, queer characters, queer histories, queer reference books, and queer creation from spaces where young people exist. There's justification to keep queer adults out of positions of influence such as teachers, coaches, and mentors. Queerness can be totally erased from youth spaces. And if young people don't ever see or experience queerness, the (faulty) logic follows that they can't *become* queer.

But young people know what they're living and experiencing. *You* know what you are living and experiencing. No matter what age you are, you know what you're feeling. You may not fully understand the intricacies and nuances of those feelings. They may still be new feelings, still in the process of forming. They may be changing and evolving as other parts of you are changing. But, regardless of that degree of uncertainty, you still know what you're feeling.

You may be young, but you're not a stranger in your own body. No one else in the world knows what it's like to inhabit your body at this stage of your life, so you are the sole authority on what's happening within you. If asexuality resonates with your experience, that should, at the very least, be respected.

It's important, though, to remain open to learning and remain willing to consider new perspectives and ideas. While no one should tell you that you aren't experiencing what you're experiencing, it's imperative that you continue to question and learn. Identity is complicated and can be a lifelong journey of discovery. While it's wonderful that you've started this journey early, you're still just at the beginning of it. Stay flexible. Stay open-minded.

Know what you know until you know something new.

What if I call myself asexual and I find out I'm wrong?

Would it make you feel better if you knew I got it wrong at first? I actually got it wrong *several* times.

The first identity label I ever used for myself, when I was in high school and still dating girls, was bisexual.

Then, when I graduated high school, I stopped calling myself bisexual and started calling myself gay.

When I realized I was somewhere on the asexual spectrum, I started calling myself graysexual.

When I realized I was confusing sensual attraction with sexual attraction, and that I never really felt sexual attraction, I started calling myself asexual instead.

I've gotten it wrong three different times, and that's just when it comes to my sexual orientation. If you throw in gender identity and romantic orientation, you'd probably get another two or three shifts from one identity marker to another.

That's a lot of change. And that's totally okay.

There's no rule in any rulebook anywhere in the world and any time in history that says that the first identity language you choose to describe yourself is the one you have to stick with *through all of time immemorial*.

Identity just doesn't work that way. People change and grow and discover new things about themselves. They evolve out of old ways of thinking and feeling. They adapt to new ideas and adopt new ways of understanding themselves. People aren't static. We *move*. That's what's cool about us.

So if today asexuality makes sense for you, don't worry about whether it's going to be true ten minutes from now or ten months from now or ten years from now. It makes sense today. It helps you today. So today...you're ace. You have every right to claim an identity that describes your experience as you understand it.

Now, there are gatekeepers out there who will try to throw up fists and shake definitions at you and say, "That's not really ace; you aren't ace unless you fit this mold or check off these five items on this asexuality checklist!" But those people don't know what they're talking about. There is no checklist. Life defies checklists. Those people have no power to tell you what is true about yourself.

If what is true today changes later, then it changes. No big deal. You discovered who you really are.

If what is true today never changes throughout the rest of your life, that's also no big deal. You discovered who you really are.

And that's what all this is fundamentally about. Discovering who you really are. We go through all this questioning and debating and pondering and worrying to be the truest version of ourselves we can be. When we know our truth and then *live* that truth, we're better able to do all of the other things we want to do in this world.

So don't worry so much about how long an identity label is going to be true. Just be sure that it *is* the truth.

Okay, that's fine and all. But seriously, how do I really know I'm truly asexual?

Alright, fine. I've been holding out on you. Here's how you know for sure you're ace.

The Office of Asexual Affairs (OAA) provides every questioning individual a brief application, the asexuality diagnostic exam in three sections (a multiple-choice section, a true/false section, and a short essay section with your choice of prompts), and a request for two valid forms of identification. Then, a certified asexuality analyst goes over your submission and determines whether or not you're truly asexual. If you are asexual, you'll receive a letter on official OAA letterhead confirming your asexuality, along with up to two coordinating microlabels, where applicable. This letter will get you into almost any asexuality meetup in the country, plus you'll get free garlic bread at Chili's on your birthday.

We all wish it was this easy. And not just for the garlic bread, either. But it's not. There is no universal answer to the question. There is no checklist. There is no diagnostic exam.

So here's the real answer to "How do I truly know I'm asexual?": You don't have to know.

You don't have to know "for sure." You're under no pressure to be totally, truly, absolutely, one hundred percent sure. Identity is complicated, and it can change over time. We can change, and how we understand our experience can change. So being totally, truly, absolutely sure is a wildly unattainable goal.

So trust yourself. Trust what you're thinking. Trust what you're feeling. Trust that how you are processing and understanding your own experience is right and fair and worth believing.

You know your own experience better than anyone. You are the authority on your own life. And you ultimately don't need anyone or anything else—not even the Office of Asexual Affairs—to confirm what you know, deep down, to be true.

What if I think I'm ace and I don't want to be?

We all have moments when we resist the truth of ourselves. We'll pretend we don't like something because other people don't think it's "cool." We'll pursue degrees or careers we don't really like because other people have certain expectations of us. We'll stick around in relationships that just aren't working because we fear we can't do better or we fear being alone. We'll deny our true gender or sexual orientation because we fear rejection, judgment, or violence.

A lot of ace folks reach a moment when they're coming to terms with who they are when they wish, very desperately, not to be ace. They reach a moment where they'll plead with whatever god or force or power in the universe they believe in, "Please, just change me. Help me change. Help me be something different. I don't want to be this. I don't want to be ace."

Unfortunately, we don't get to do that. We don't get to change. We can pretend we're something different. We can live our lives going through the motions of the life we'd rather have, but it's much like wearing a coat that doesn't fit. Yeah, you've got the coat on. But you can hardly move in it, it doesn't zip up all the way, and in the end, it doesn't help you or keep you warm at all.

We can't change the fact that we're asexual. But we can change the way we treat ourselves because of it.

The first step is recognizing where our negative feelings about asexuality come from. From the very start of our lives, we live under the massive pressure of cultural expectations. There are expectations about how we inhabit our bodies, how we inhabit our genders, how we relate to other people, how we build relationships, and how we share our bodies with other people. And these expectations are the same for everyone around us. We all live under these cultural expectations.

For people whose bodies, lives, and desires fit these cultural expectations, life is pretty easy. They're following "the rules," and the culture, in return, designates their lives as good and normal.

For people whose bodies, lives, and desires deviate from these cultural expectations, life is a lot harder. Those people who are living in defiance of "the rules" are designated as abnormal, wrong, bad, and the culture wants to make sure they're punished for it. And the other people—the ones lucky enough to fit the expectations—are encouraged and rewarded for reinforcing that punishment through insults, social marginalization, or worse.

Asexuality sits outside of the cultural expectations we live under. Therefore throughout our lives, whether we recognize it or not, we have absorbed messages that asexuality is bad, wrong, and abnormal. And unless we've had some miraculous intervention by the asexuality gods, those negative messages are all we've ever known about asexuality. So when we start to recognize asexuality in us, we believe it is what the culture has told us about it.

But none of those messages—that asexuals are broken or deficient or lacking something essential that everyone else has—are true. Asexuality is a perfectly normal, perfectly acceptable, and perfectly valid human experience. The only negative thing about asexuality is that there are mistruths that we believe about it.

So when we are struggling with accepting our asexuality, we have to separate the identity from the ideas around it. We have to toss out the negative ideas about asexuality. They don't serve us. We have to keep the asexuality. It's part of us. A wonderful part. And we should take care of it.

We have to replace that question—"How can I not be ace?"—with better questions for ourselves: "How can I treat myself with love and kindness?" "How can I better accept myself for who I am?" "How can I learn to love who I am?"

That's the kind of change we should be asking of ourselves. It's hard work, to be sure. But the hard work is worth it. And you deserve that work. You deserve that self-love and self-acceptance.

PART II

Asexuality and Others

Chapter 5

HOW DO I COME OUT AS ASEXUAL?

I'm in a polyamorous relationship with my husband, Neil, and my partner, Scott. (More on relationships while ace in Chapters 7 and 8.)

Scott is an astrophysicist, and his scientific focus is the search for exoplanets. He's spent his career looking out beyond the edges of our solar system to find other planets circling other stars millions of miles away. He's discovered a couple (which is a very cool thing to drop into a conversation about what you do for work), and he once told me what it feels like to discover a planet previously unknown by any human in the universe.

"There's a moment that feels completely unbelievable and overwhelming," he told me. "You, alone, know something that no one else in the world knows. You know about this planet. Just you. And this knowledge is going to add to our understanding of the universe, which is a big thing. For a couple of minutes, you're the only person who knows the universe this way. It's so exciting, having that knowledge, and you're in that excitement for the first five minutes.

But then there's the sixth minute, and something new comes in. You feel anxious, scared a little. A lot, even. Because now, you have to share this incredible discovery with other people. They're going to respond. Some are going to cheer for the news. Some are going to question it. See, it's not a changed universe that's scary. What's scary is just...other people."

73

Asexuality isn't astrophysics, but we go through something similar when we are discovering who we are. When our identity is just ours, when we are the only ones in the universe who know, the feeling can be euphoric. We make sense to ourselves. We're empowered by that knowledge. All of the parts of us click into place, and just like Scott discovering a planet, for a little while, we know ourselves in a way no other person does. We know ourselves more completely, more authentically.

But then, it's our sixth minute, and the implications of knowing this complete, authentic version of ourselves creep in. In order for the people we care about to know us the way we now know us, we have to tell them. We've got to show them this new version of ourselves.

We face an important choice: Should I come out?

Coming out is scary. It invites a kind of scrutiny that can be difficult to deal with. We open ourselves up to other people's misconceptions, to their lack of understanding, to their bigotry. We can experience confusion, self-doubt, and shame. Coming out can fundamentally change our relationships with certain people, and sometimes even end them. And, worst of all, coming out can sometimes invite more serious harm—being kicked out of the house, being verbally or emotionally abused, or experiencing violence.

This chapter is about coming out: how to decide if and when it's right to come out and how to do it safely and successfully. You've already done the really hard part. You've figured out your identity. Throughout this chapter, we'll discuss ways to make coming out as ace to the people in your life a positive next step. We'll talk about timing. We'll talk about finding the right words. We'll talk about dealing with less than desirable responses. We'll make sure you go into your coming-out process with the confidence you need to nail it.

Do I have to come out?

Let's get this out of the way right from the beginning: You don't have to come out.

There's a lot of pressure in queer communities for individuals to be visible, out, and proud. We'll discuss the reasons in this chapter—and they're really good reasons—but there is no requirement that you, as an individual who's discovered their asexuality, must also be out as ace.

For many people, the journey of self-discovery is an interior journey. It's a process that happens within themselves, and it's not a journey they share with the outside world. This is perfectly okay. We are not obligated to share certain truths of our identities in order to be considered legitimate. Our truth doesn't become a lie simply because we keep it to ourselves.

The journey of self-discovery isn't universal for everyone. That journey doesn't require specific steps to be valid. And your journey doesn't have to match someone else's to be considered "right." If you choose to make your relationship with your asexuality a private one or one that's only shared with your closest of relationships, that's great. That's your relationship to your asexuality. It doesn't make that relationship any less true, and it doesn't make you any less ace.

There's also no rush to come out. Recognizing and personally embracing your asexuality won't activate some alarm that sends the Ace Police to your house to usher you out of the closet. You control the parameters of your relationship with your asexuality, and that includes when you share your truth with others. If you want to keep it private for a while and come out sometime later, that's great. If you want to come out immediately and shout it from the rooftops, that's great, too. And you can always decide that the timing will never be right and you won't ever come out. But the decision is yours. You don't have a ticking clock to keep up with. You don't have a deadline to hit. The timing is completely up to you.

Why does coming out matter?

I have always been a really strong advocate of coming out. I've come out twice in my life: I came out as gay when I was 18, and I came out as asexual when I was 42. Both coming-out experiences were challenging, but ultimately both experiences helped me become a stronger, happier, and more complete version of myself. I've twice lived the benefits of coming out, and while I know it's not a universally held or desired experience, I think there are two main benefits to coming out.

Coming out celebrates who you are

When I was 18 and deciding whether or not to come out to my parents as gay, I was leaning heavily toward not coming out. I grew up in a very small, very conservative rural town in the Deep South. For most of my adolescence, I didn't know anyone who was gay, and the only stories I'd heard about gay people were stories of how they'd been ostracized by their families (rightfully, by the family's standards) and doomed to live miserable lives, alone and unhappy.

I didn't want that. I had a very loving relationship with my parents. They were supportive and encouraging. And while I didn't have confirmation that they were homophobic (I'd never heard them say anything about homosexuality one way or the other, supportive or damning), I knew what the messages were in the world around me. They couldn't possibly accept a son who was gay.

James, a very gay, very hilarious actor I met during my first semester studying theater in college, wanted me to change my mind. "But if you don't tell them who you are, then who is it they're loving and supporting?" James thought it was a terrible idea for me to stay in the closet. "If you don't tell them, you're letting your parents love an illusion. And if you let them love an illusion, you are deciding you want to *live* an illusion. And let me tell you something. That is a miserable existence. And you aren't that good an actor."

James had come out of the closet at 14, which was sort of a miracle and an unbelievable act of courage. He was from an even smaller and more conservative town than I was, but he was completely unafraid to let every part of him shine. He was unapologetically gay, unapologetically feminine, and unapologetically loud about it. He didn't live an illusion. He just lived his truth.

And James was right. When we choose to stay in the closet, we're agreeing to let the world know and love a version of ourselves that's constructed, made up, an illusion. When we do that, when we agree to this edited, sanitized version of ourselves, we're cutting off the air to all the truest parts of ourselves, the parts that make us uniquely who we are.

Those parts may confuse the world. Those parts may make the world angry. Those parts may be considered wrong, broken, blasphemous, imaginary, sinful, scary, or illegal. But when those parts of us shine, they shine. They're the *truth*.

That's why it can be so important to come out, even when it feels like it'd be easier to stay in the closet. You deserve to live the truth of your life. You deserve to shine as brightly as you can.

The world may give you a hard time, but stepping into the world as everything you are, everything you can be, and everything you *will* be can be absolutely worth it.

Coming out helps other people see themselves

You might think after being out as a gay person for 20 years, when I discovered I was asexual at 42, I'd be equally open as an ace person.

You'd be wrong.

When I first recognized and accepted my asexuality, I didn't really tell anyone. I told the people closest to me—my husband, my best friend, a few trusted queer confidants—but I was very uncomfortable being public about it.

I didn't think it mattered much. It's not like anyone thought I was straight. I'd been openly gay for my whole adult life, so this change, from "gay" to "asexual," didn't feel like an important enough shift to make. It didn't feel like a major revelation. I was just changing the flavor of queer I was.

This was, of course, simply justifying my fear. My fear of rejection. My fear of ridicule. My fear of the people I loved changing the way they looked at me or treated me. Even a healthy dose of fear that being ace would end my relationships.

Not coming out was an easy way to avoid all of that. So I kept quiet.

I and the people who meant the most to me were comfortable with my asexuality. I wasn't lying about it. I just had the volume on it way, way down. I'd share articles about asexuality here and there on social media. And I'd talk about asexuality online—never directly referring to myself that way—and that felt like enough.

Then, I got a message on Facebook from a college friend I hadn't heard from in years.

> *Hey. I know it's been a while, but I just wanted to share something. I saw those asexuality articles you posted, and it got me thinking. I think I'm gray-ace. I don't know if you shared them because you're ace or because you just thought they were interesting, but I'm happy you shared them. It made a lot of things about myself clearer. It really helped me out. I don't think I'd have found this if you hadn't shared something about it. So, again: thanks.*

I immediately messaged him back, telling him I was ace and not just an ally. I offered him a friendly shoulder anytime he wanted to talk. And I stopped being scared and started sharing my identity a lot more in public.

In that one message, my college friend reminded me of something I'd known for 20 years, something I learned when I started being vocally queer in my early twenties: You can't be it if you don't see it.

Being out doesn't just announce who you are to the world. It also announces what's possible for others. When you are out as an asexual person, you're sending a message that says, "Hey, look, someone like me, who looks like me, who lives my kind of life, who's happy and okay, is an asexual person." You demonstrate what you are and what is possible.

Coming out doesn't just allow you to live your truth. It creates a space where living a truth like yours becomes possible for someone else. When we come out and let our true selves shine, that light sometimes reaches people who are still in the dark about themselves.

Our light, our shine helps them see themselves. It gives them permission to shine as well.

And in a world where visible representations of asexual people are really hard to come by, the power you have as an out individual is enormous. You might be the only asexual person someone else has ever met or seen. You might be the first person to clearly explain the ace experience to someone. Your visibility might change the way someone else sees their own identity. That's *big*.

While it's great to have visible ace representation in mainstream movies, books, and TV shows, the visibility of individual ace people in their personal human networks has a profound impact on the community. We change the world for ace folks one person at a time.

It might not seem like much, but it's a superpower.

So I've decided to come out. How do I know it's the right time?

Wouldn't it be great if I could just tell you, with extreme confidence, exactly when a person should come out of the closet? Or if I could just share an algorithm with you that would calculate with precision the optimal time to reveal who you are?

No such confidence and no such algorithm exists, unfortunately. Coming out is a highly individual process, specific to the person and the community support structures around them. The best answer one can give—an answer that's really unsatisfying—is "It's the right time when it's the right time."

But that unsatisfying answer is important to think about. We put a lot of pressure on ourselves when figuring out our identity and deciding when to share that identity with others to "get it right." We have to get the language right. We have to get the timing right. We have to make sure we are understanding our experience the right way. We have to make sure we'll be right tomorrow, the next day, ten years into the future. We demand so much "rightness" of ourselves when exploring our identity that we sometimes put more focus on the "rightness" than on us.

We deserve to think about ourselves, our identity, and the way we share those things with others without all that pressure. We deserve to explore our asexuality without the voice in the back of our heads screaming, "BUT ARE YOU RIGHT? ARE YOU SURE?" We deserve room to make mistakes, change our minds, evolve, and grow.

So while I can't—and won't—provide a concrete answer to "How do I know it's the right time to come out?," I will say this: The right time to come out is whenever you're ready. Maybe you're ready right now. Maybe you'll be ready a few months down the road. Maybe you'll never be ready. All are valid. All are okay.

Your readiness, your comfort, your confidence are the only things that make it the "right" time to come out.

So how do I know if I'm ready to come out?

Okay, now this is something we can dig into.

There are three main components to being ready to come out: knowing why you're coming out, knowing it's safe to come out, and knowing how you're going to come out.

Once you have a handle on all three, you will most likely be in the right place to share your asexuality with other people.

Let's take them one by one.

Why am I coming out?
Coming out is a bit like an identity magic trick.

You begin with something private: in this case, your asexuality. It's something you hold within you, something that only you have considered and cultivated.

But with a flash of light or a flourish of your hands and a couple of magic words—"I'm asexual!"—spoken to one other person in the world, the private becomes public. Your asexuality is transformed. It exists in the world. It bumps up against other people and their preconceived notions, against culture, its structures, and the biases those structures hold.

That's a huge transformation.

Whether private or public, your identity is valid. It's valid because it's yours. So coming out doesn't validate your identity. The choice to come out is not about affirming who you are. It's a choice to transform your truth into something that exists beyond the bounds of yourself.

So it's important to know *why* you want to do that.

Do you want to come out because you feel as though you have to? Do you believe your asexuality isn't "real" until you're out as ace publicly? Do you think you can't be truly ace until you're out of the closet? Do you feel like a fake or a liar or a cheat if you're not out of the closet? Do you feel as though you're letting down other ace people if you don't come out?

If these are the "whys" motivating your desire to come out, I'd recommend you reconsider. These reasons are all about other people and the way their perception of you defines who you are. All of that energy is directed outward, directed away from you. It measures the success or failure of a coming out by the responses of other people. It's all in their hands. Someone else is in control of your destiny.

I hate that. I think it misses the point of coming out entirely.

Coming out is something we do for ourselves. It's a choice we make to share what we know about ourselves with other people. We're giving someone a gift when we come out; we're saying, "Hey. I think you're important enough to know me at my most vulnerable, my most truthful. I'm giving you a part of myself that I don't entrust to everyone." We come out because we want to be seen. We come out because we want to be known. We come out because we want to move through the world as everything we know ourselves to be.

All of that is about us. About you. What you want and what you need. That's how coming out should be. Coming out should be about you.

Do you want to come out because you're proud of your asexuality? Do you want to come out because you want your friends and family to know the truest version of you? Are you tired of not living your truth out loud?

These reasons are about you. These reasons provide a strong foundation for living your best ace life.

So ask yourself: Who am I coming out for? If the answer is anyone or anything but you... It might not be the right time. If the answer is you... Watch out world, here you come.

Is it safe to come out?

You don't owe anyone your coming out. Anyone. Not your friends. Not your family. Not anyone. Coming out is a choice you make for yourself, when you're ready. So if it's not safe yet for you to come out—if coming out could mean physical harm, emotional harm, mental harm; if coming out means you'll get kicked out, or cut off financially, or cut off from relationships that mean a lot to you—you don't have to come out.

Remember, this is for you, and we don't do things that put us in harm's way. You don't let anyone down by protecting yourself. And you don't let your identity down either. Safety first. You have to prioritize safety. You can't let your big ace energy shine bright when you're swatting off harm.

We prioritize safety because when we come out, we're letting a beautiful, vulnerable part of ourselves step outside for the first time. Make sure that part of you gets to step into the sunshine. Not a rainstorm.

It deserves that. You deserve that.

Be in control of how you come out

Do you know how I told my parents I was gay? I wrote a letter.

I wasn't living at home at the time, so I went to their house when I knew they were out running errands, and I left the letter I'd written—a three-page, handwritten letter on loose-leaf paper—on the kitchen counter.

Some of my friends think I'm crazy for doing this, but I feel as though I have to. I believe that you both love me very much and trust my judgment. I hope you understand that I'm doing this only because I love you and because I want you to understand my life. This has taken me a year and a half to work out in my own heart and mind, and I need you both to know what I've known all this time: I am gay.

I'm sorry. Not for what I am, but for how you must feel. I can understand it—disgust, shame, embarrassment—because for most of my life I've felt it, too. But I've finally reached a point in my life where what I am is something I can accept and be proud of. It has been a victory for me, and I hope you both can share in that victory.

(I still have the letter. My mom kept it, and I read it again for the first time when I started writing this book. Eighteen-year-old Cody was a lot braver than I am now most days.)

I left it on the counter, and I bolted, waiting for their response with my heart and stomach wedged anxiously in my throat.

Things turned out great. They totally accepted me and loved their freshly minted gay son. But that's how I felt in control of coming out. I knew I was going to be too scared to actually say the words in person. I'd stumble and backtrack. Or I'd simply not say anything and chicken out completely. A letter wouldn't stumble. A letter wouldn't chicken out. A letter would let me say all the things I wanted and *needed* to say. It wasn't just important for me to have my queerness to share. It was also important that I was able to share it *on my own terms.*

Come out on *your* terms. Maybe that means coming out in private one-on-ones with the important people in your life. Maybe that means sharing your truth over dinner with family and friends. Maybe that means making a coming-out video or a coming-out post to share on social media. Maybe that means writing a letter and leaving it on the kitchen counter.

But your terms matter. The how, the who, the when, and the why matter. And you should be the one deciding what those are. Choose the terms that make you feel safe. Choose the terms that make you feel empowered.

What happens when coming out isn't in my control?

Sometimes, our coming out happens with someone else in the driver's seat. A friend you shared your truth with shares that with someone else without your permission. Someone sends a private socialmedia post to your parents before you're ready to tell them. Your mom tells the extended family even though you wanted to keep them out of your trusted circle for a while. Sometimes the outing is accidental and done without intentional malice. Other times, it's purposeful and intended to cause harm.

Being outed, whether intentional or not, is never okay. The feelings of betrayal, embarrassment, anger, fear, or shame that come up as a result are all valid responses to something so personal being taken from your control. You may be told you should just "get over it." You may be told you're being too sensitive, since it's the truth. Particularly vicious people might even tell you that you deserve to be outed. None of these things are true. They're excuses and deflections to neglect assuming responsibility for causing you harm.

If you find yourself in a situation where your asexuality is made public or shared with people before you're ready, know that you are not to blame. Coming out is an experience that should belong to you and you alone, and if that's taken away from you, full responsibility lies in the hands of the person who took it.

It won't be fun. There are going to be plenty of negative feelings in the wake of being outed. But don't let those negative feelings become part of how you feel about your asexuality. Your control and your autonomy may be taken from you, but don't let your pride in yourself or your empowerment go with them.

I'm afraid my parents are going to react badly to my being asexual. What do I do?

Coming out to your parents can be really difficult. They're the people you're closest to, and they can often be the people who put up the most resistance to the new way we understand ourselves. They can end up saying the harshest things. They can make us feel the most insecure, the worst about ourselves.

But it's important to remember that, most of the time, parents behave that way because they're going through something, too.

Our parents meet us at a really weird time in our lives, when we're nothing but a little flesh blob of crying and pooping and throwing up. They meet us when we're not even ourselves yet. And they know us for years like this. *Years.*

They have all this time to invent who we are. Who they hope we are. They decide our careers. They figure out how many kids we'll have and where we'll live, how often we'll visit, and what family celebrations will be like. They know us as a person built out of their hopes and dreams, their expectations about what we'll be and what we'll do. The us our parents grow to love at first is a person who doesn't wholly exist.

When we come out as ace or queer or trans—whatever we end up being that wasn't part of their original plan—we change their understanding of the person they've known and loved for years. When we come out, we're asking them to meet someone totally new, someone they were not expecting. And that can be hard.

We experience something similar when we're coming to terms with ourselves. Remember how hard it was to finally say to yourself, "I'm asexual?" Remember all of the feelings you had? All the internal conflict? You had to give up this imagined version of yourself, too, so that you could accept yourself as you truly are. That wasn't easy either. They're going through something similar.

Now I'm not saying you should allow your parents to treat you poorly. Not at all. We deserve respect and kindness and support and love from the people we're closest to. But we can also extend some compassion for what we're asking them to give up. We know they're getting an incredible, much better, asexual version of ourselves. It may just take a second for them to catch up.

Coming out is a process

While I didn't come out officially until I was 18, I knew I was queer when I was 15. Or mostly knew. I kept waffling back and forth. But I knew *something* was up, even if I wasn't ready yet to commit to it fully.

I remember the very first time I was going to tell another human being that I was queer. It was my friend Amanda. I was doing it over the phone (because she and I would talk on the phone almost every night), and I was so scared. I could barely breathe. My hands were shaking. I had written out what I was going to say to her, and the paper I'd written it down on was wrinkled and a mess because I'd been clutching it so tightly for the whole afternoon.

And finally it was time. It was time to tell her. It was time to come out. And I did it. I told her.

"Amanda, you know... I think... I think I'm kinda gay."

And I had one second of feeling completely triumphant. Courageous. I had scaled Mount Everest and I was standing at the peak, surveying the glorious world beneath my feet.

And the next second I realized, "Oh no. I have to do this like a hundred more times for everyone else in my life."

We tend to think of coming out as a one-night-only, very special episode kind of event. One and done. We invest a lot of energy and fear and anxiety in that very first time, as though it's the only time we'll ever have to come out. And we put a lot of pressure on ourselves to make that very first time perfect. We have to say the perfect thing. We have to perfectly understand every nuance of our identity. We have to project the perfect amount of confidence. We have to be perfectly whatever it is we're telling someone we are.

But coming out is a process. We come out over and over again. We come out to our friends. To our families. To our coworkers. To the people we share hobbies with. To the folks we volunteer with. And throughout our lives we keep coming out. We change jobs. We move. We take up new hobbies. We make new friends.

You never stop coming out. So the pressure we put on ourselves to make our coming out perfect is misguided. Only practice makes perfect, and trust me, when it comes to coming out, you're gonna get a lot of practice.

Think of each coming out as a step forward. Not the final destination. Maybe this time you get the words a little wrong. No sweat. There's next time. Maybe you learn a little bit more about asexuality that helps you realize you're more demi than gray. Cool. The next time you come out, you'll be able to share yourself more clearly.

Think of coming out as a lifelong process of sharing who you are with the world. And because you are a complex and amazing human being, the story of who you are can't be told in one sitting.

No pressure to be perfect. Just be you. Each and every time.

Find the joy in being who you are

You know what we don't say often enough? Being asexual is awesome.

I find a lot of joy in my asexuality. I experience the world in a unique way. When I think about attraction, it has all these different dimensions that have nothing to do with sex. My asexuality has helped me understand myself more completely. And ultimately, it's my asexuality that's connected me with all of you, my community, my big, chaotic ace family. There's a lot of joy there.

It took a while to get there. I had to do a lot of work on myself to be able to say that honestly. But I experience a lot of very joyful moments because of, not in spite of, being ace. Find that joy in being who you are. You're not going to get rid of the nerves or the fear or the uncertainty. They're along for the ride. But you can make sure they're riding shotgun to joy.

Because you'd never have gotten to the point of coming out if you hadn't experienced joy. The joy of finding a language for who you are. The joy of realizing you aren't broken or deficient or wrong—just ace. The joy of knowing you aren't alone in the world, that there's a whole community of people who experience the world the way you do. You have to feel and know that joy before you can even *think* about coming out. So remember it. Hold on to it. Let it be the fuel that propels you into your new life.

Coming out means stepping into the world as someone new. There's so much possibility in that. There's so much possibility in *you*.

You deserve a coming-out experience that reflects that.

Chapter 6

HOW DO I DEAL WITH MICROAGGRESSIONS?

"So, this is gonna go nowhere, right?"

I'm on a date, and the man across the table from me is confused, maybe even coming off a little angry. We're having coffee. We've gotten past the basics—*What do you do? What kind of music do you like? Have you seen...?*—and it's going really well. He's cute. We have chemistry. And he isn't even put off by the fact that I have multiple partners and am polyamorous.

So, it's time. It's the point where I make sure it's clear to this person I'm connecting with that I am asexual. Not as an apology or a disclaimer. I want to make sure he's seeing me for who I am, that I am putting all my cards on the table.

And this—"So, this is gonna go nowhere, right?"—is his response.

"Well, whether or not this 'goes someplace' is up for discussion," I say. "I think we're getting along pretty well—"

"No, the asexual thing." He says it with some disdain in his voice. "This can't go anywhere because you're...like *that*."

I sit up a little straighter in my chair and take a deep breath. I can feel something hot start to twist in my chest, radiating up into my cheeks, holding back any words. It's how my body feels shame.

I guess he picks up on the shift in my demeanor, because he immediately starts to tumble over words. "No, no. Like...that's not how

I mean for that to come off. You're just... It surprised me. I just think you're really handsome, so how can you be asexual, you know? Such a waste."

Inside, I feel a rant brewing. *No. I don't think it's a waste. And I don't know why me being handsome or not should have anything to do with me being ace. And for you to just dismiss me as a dead end just because I'm ace is... That's such a negative... Look, just say you don't understand asexuality instead of making these sweeping—and wrong!—generalizations about me.*

The rant stays stuck in my head, because the shame I'm feeling is the only thing I can focus on. I don't say anything. I breathe and give a little self-deprecating shrug.

"You're not offended, are you?" he says. "I said you were handsome. I was paying you a compliment."

"Right," I say.

"Maybe you should give me a shot sometime," he says. "Maybe I can fix that whole ace thing for you. Show you what you're missing."

This guy wasn't unique in his attitude. I've been on plenty of dates since coming out as asexual that have followed this routine. Things are going well. There's chemistry. It feels like we both are excited about the possibilities. I say I'm ace.

Record scratch. The chemistry evaporates. I want to run. And it's always accompanied by the seemingly innocuous throwaway comments that sometimes sound like compliments but always feel like daggers.

You don't have to be on a date to experience these, either. They can show up anywhere. An encouraging word from a parent that makes you feel worse than before. A "pep talk" from a friend that feels more invalidating than encouraging. An offhand comment by a teacher or mentor that makes you question whether or not you really know yourself and your own experience.

Navigating the obstacles of figuring out your identity and coming out can feel like the end of a journey, but those steps really mark an important beginning. You, as an ace person, have to exist in the world.

Who you are and what that means will brush up against the prejudices, stereotypes, and preconceived notions of other people. That point of contact can be a place of friction, and without the right mindset for dealing with it, that friction could sow doubt, insecurity, and shame in you.

This chapter is all about microaggressions, those innocuous throwaway comments that sometimes sound like compliments but always feel like daggers. We'll explore what they are and why they exist. And we'll come up with ways to encounter them that don't leave lasting wounds.

What are microaggressions?

Microaggressions are everyday words, actions, or situations that, whether intentional or not, communicate negative and derogatory messages to a person based on their membership in a marginalized group. Microaggressions focus on some part of your identity—your gender, your race, your sexual orientation, your disability—and use the harmful stereotypes of that identity to communicate something negative *about* you *to* you.

Sometimes, they're more direct, and they feel like insults or jabs. Other times, microaggressions are much more subtle. They're wrapped in the guise of a compliment, or they're spoken in a very offhand manner. But microaggressions always reveal some bias against a person's identity group, and they make a person feel uncomfortable, hurt, insulted, or diminished.

That quality of microaggressions—their subtlety—is part of what makes them so negatively impactful. When you experience a microaggression, the hurt and discomfort you feel is very real. But it's happening in what feels like a very ordinary situation. "It's *just* a joke." "It's *just* a compliment." "It's *just* a suggestion." "I'm *just* trying to help you." That ordinariness can make you feel like you've misread the situation, like you're making it up, like the hurt you feel isn't earned or true. Even though you know what you're experiencing.

That's why it's important to think about microaggressions and learn to recognize them. It's very easy for us to internalize the negative ideas they carry, to believe the harmful things they communicate about us. Knowing a microaggression when we see one helps us steer clear of internalizing its negative messages.

Am I just being too sensitive about these comments? Are they really that bad?

Even though microaggressions are often small in scope—a casual comment, a joke, an unintended action—they can have powerful and lasting impacts on the people who experience them.

Microaggressions create deep discomfort and hurt in otherwise average and everyday interactions: a dinner with your family, a conversation with a friend, a work session with a teacher, or a meeting with a coworker. These environments and interactions should feel easy and safe, but microaggressions turn them into hostile ground. When you can no longer rely on the people and spaces you consider safe to be safe, that can take a heavy emotional and psychological toll.

What's more, microaggressions do this without calling much attention to themselves. As we said before, they can be very subtle, only raising red flags in the individuals being targeted. Other people don't necessarily notice the harm happening. These spaces remain safe and easy for everyone else. This isolation, being *alone* in this experience of harm, compounds the damage.

Microaggressions also inflict harm due to their frequency. These are not big, bold, once-in-a-lifetime expressions of hate or discrimination. Microaggressions, due to their size and subtlety, happen again and again, in many different contexts. Remember, they happen in everyday situations, so it's not uncommon to experience them *every day*. The impact of microaggressions accumulates over time, adding up to intense mental and emotional stress, which can bubble over into issues with your physical health.

Microaggressions are like death by a thousand cuts.

Examples of microaggressions

This is not an exhaustive list of asexual microaggressions, but what
follows includes many of the most common ones. We'll look at them
one by one, break down what stereotypes form the foundation of each
microaggression, and explore why each microaggression fails to reflect
the truth of asexuality. Where appropriate, I'll include some ways to
respond to these microaggressions when you experience them in the
world.

This chapter won't erase the hurt microaggressions cause, but it will
(hopefully) give you some added armor to stand up to them.

"So you're a plant/amoeba/robot?"
You'd be hard-pressed to find an asexual person who hasn't run into
this at least once in their interactions with other people. It's often
delivered as just a cute little joke, a fun little play on words that doesn't
mean any harm.

But this microaggression is more than just a play on words. This
microaggression is dehumanizing. It paints asexuality as something
that couldn't possibly happen to a living, breathing *person*. It could
only happen to plants or microorganisms or machines. It paints you as
someone who's having an experience that's less than human.

Asexuality is a human experience. Full stop. Period. Your asexuality
doesn't make you a plant or an amoeba or a robot. Any suggestion that
it does is misguided and wrong.

"But I just meant it as a joke." Jokes that diminish the essential
humanity of a person aren't funny, and the intention behind a
comment or joke doesn't change the impact of it. If you find it hurtful, it
doesn't matter if it was meant in humor.

"But that's what 'asexual' means. The dictionary says..." Hauling out
the dictionary and arguing semantics is a disingenuous way to shut
down conversation. Sure, "asexual" is a term that describes a way
plants and single-cell organisms reproduce. But language is fluid and

evolving, and "asexual" also refers to our very human experience. Don't internalize someone's bad-faith argument.

"You've got to be a plant/amoeba/robot if you don't want sex. Everyone wants sex." We'll get into this more deeply in later chapters, but the idea that everyone wants sex is simply wrong. There is no universal human rule when it comes to sex. We can experience desire, attraction, and intimacy in a wide variety of ways, including not experiencing them at all. All of it is valid. All of it is *human*.

"You can't be asexual. Asexuality isn't a real thing."
When confronted with an experience that's unfamiliar or difficult to understand, the path of least resistance is to dismiss it, to discount its reality.

This microaggression is hung on that idea that everyone must desire sex. It's built on the idea that experiencing sexual attraction and desiring sexual intimacy are things we all share, things we all do by default. When confronted with someone who breaks that norm, some people find it easier to call that person's experience a fiction instead of altering their understanding of the world to include something new.

Are there more allosexual people than asexual people? Sure. But quantity doesn't determine validity. Just because the asexual experience is less common doesn't mean it's fabricated. Just because most people are allosexual doesn't mean allosexuality is the only "real" sexual orientation.

Asexuality is real. Asexual people exist. You and your experience occupy space in this world, and no one can take that fact from you.

"This is just a phase you're going through."
This microaggression is not one we hear only from other people. It's one we often inflict on ourselves.

It's an extension of the "asexuality isn't real" microaggression, an attempt to diminish and dismiss the validity of asexuality. Reducing asexuality to a phase is supposing asexuality is a passing whim, an occasional fascination, something more like a hobby. And these sorts of transitional experiences don't have to be taken seriously. They don't have to be respected. Thinking of asexuality as a phase reinforces the belief that it can't be a real and valid human experience. It reinforces the idea that asexuality is a deviation, a fragmentation of "real" sexuality.

This microaggression also suggests that we, as asexual people, can simply decide to stop being asexual. If asexuality is "just a phase," then it's not a lived-in and authentic experience. It's no more than a coat we can try on or take off as we wish.

Asexuality is not something we make up. Asexuality is not a choice we make. Asexuality is a real experience, and while identity can shift and change over time, it is not "just a phase."

This microaggression takes on a different flavor when we're the ones using it on ourselves.

When we think of our own asexuality as "just a phase," we're often doing so in the hopes that we can change it, remove it, make it go away. If it's "just a phase," then something can change it: a doctor, a partner, a new mindset, sheer will. We're deflecting the work of facing ourselves.

It can sometimes feel safer or easier to deny our reality. "It's just a phase" can feel like an answer. But eventually, the truth catches up to us, and we can only become the best version of ourselves when we acknowledge and love the full truth of who we are. Eventually, we have to admit that it's not "just a phase." It's who we are.

"You're too nice/handsome/smart/pretty to be asexual."
The microaggressions that sometimes cut the deepest are those that, on the surface, appear to be complimentary. What's the problem with being told you're nice or smart? What's the issue with being told you're pretty or handsome?

This microaggression is rooted in the idea that asexual people, because they don't experience sexual attraction, should not possess qualities that would attract allosexual people to them. If we aren't going to want sex or if we aren't going to find others sexually attractive, then we should erase ourselves from the allosexual gaze as much as possible: don't be attractive, don't be smart, don't be kind, don't be interesting. We can't be attractive if sex isn't going to be an option, and if we are attractive in some way, we're playing the game unfairly or existing in a way that's incomprehensible.

The idea that asexual people are "blank slates"—that because we don't experience sexual attraction we are also lacking personality, are aesthetically unappealing, and are uninterested in other kinds of human connection—is a pervasive one. But you don't have to dull your shine simply because you're ace.

You can be ace and attractive. You can be ace and fashionable. You can be ace and have an electric personality. You can be ace and be the center of attention in any room you enter. You're never "too" anything simply because you're ace.

"Maybe your standards are just too high."

This microaggression is rooted in the idea that asexuality is something we choose, not something we are.

Because sexual attraction is considered a universal experience, if you're not wanting sex or not experiencing sexual attraction, it's assumed to be due to some problem in you. This microaggression—"your standards are too high!"—locates that problem in the choices you make. If you just loosened your standards or if you didn't expect so much, then you'd be able to attract someone more readily. If your standards were lowered, you wouldn't need to be asexual as a cover.

Asexuality is not an excuse we make or a justification we produce for unrealistically high standards in a partner.

"Maybe you should see a doctor/see a therapist/ get your hormones checked."

Another way people deny the naturalness of asexuality as an experience of the world is to dismiss it as a physical ailment or mental condition.

We're dealing again with the cultural idea that experiencing sexual attraction is a universal human experience, and if you're not experiencing it, something is wrong with you. This family of microaggressions locates that "something is wrong" in your body or your mind. It pathologizes asexuality.

Asexuality is not a pathology. It is not a medical condition. It is not a hormone imbalance. It is not a mental disorder. It is not the result of anxiety, stress, or depression. Asexuality is as natural a sexual orientation as any of the allosexual identities. Asexuality does not mean there is something wrong with you.

While all microaggressions cause harm, there's a particular harm caused by this family of microaggressions that's important to discuss. Internalizing the sentiments peddled by comments like these will send healthy asexual people to seek out medical or psychiatric help. But it's unfortunately likely that the doctor or mental health professional they see won't be aware of or know enough about asexuality to properly consult the asexual person.

Asexual people are often unnecessarily medicalized due to this lack of awareness. They will be prescribed drugs or put on hormone treatments, and they'll be put through tests or regularly attend therapy, all for something that requires none of those things. This overmedicalization can cause a whole new set of issues for the asexual person, deepening their feelings of shame or brokenness when these "treatments" fail to solve the "problem."

Medical professionals and mental health professionals should consider asexuality as normal and healthy as any other sexual orientation. If your doctor or therapist insists on treating your asexuality as a symptom of a problem instead of an authentic part of who you are, the care you're receiving is doing more harm than good. Your asexuality exists because it's a part of who you are. It doesn't exist because there's something broken in you that requires medical intervention.

But don't some people have low hormone levels or hangups about sex? Sure. Low libido, hormone deficiencies, and mental blocks about sex and relationships exist. They're real problems that do require intervention. But it should not be an automatic assumption that a person's belief or growing understanding that they're asexual is related to one of these conditions.

Medical professionals (and, honestly, the people in our lives who love and support us) shouldn't make asexuality a thing we believe once everything else is ruled out. That's a grueling and painful process to put a person through. Some people are ace. That's how their bodies and minds work. There's nothing wrong with it.

"You're too young to be asexual."

In my work as an asexuality educator and content creator, I hear from young people all the time worrying about whether they're too young to know they're ace. They feel ace. Descriptions of ace lives and stories of ace people resonate deeply with them. They feel they're not like their peers in a fundamental way, and asexuality comes closest to describing that difference for them. But they second guess themselves, because someone in their life told them, "You're too young to know that."

Almost every queer person I know—myself included—knew from a very early age they weren't like other people. I knew as early as fourth or fifth grade that I wasn't like the boys in my class and that I was different from them. I didn't know how. I didn't have words for it. But I *knew* something in me wasn't in them, and vice versa. I have transgender friends, nonbinary friends, bisexual friends, lesbian friends, pansexual friends, asexual friends, and aromantic friends who all tell a version of this about themselves. A lot of us clue into our differences as children.

So the idea that asexuality or queerness of any kind can only be real or true if you're an adult is a strange one. We don't make the same assumption of allosexual or non-queer children. We accept—and encourage—their crushes, pairing off, dating, and the like. But queerness, in this strange conception of the world, like an unlocked level in a video game, can only happen when someone hits the arbitrary age we've decided makes them an adult.

It just doesn't work that way. You're not too young to know what's going on inside you. You're not too young to know what you're feeling or what you're experiencing. It's okay to explore asexuality as an identity as a young person if it speaks to how you feel and what you experience.

Does it mean you're ace forever? No. None of us can be sure we'll be ace forever. Identity is fluid and can evolve over our lifetimes. But don't let anyone tell you that you're too young to know yourself, at this moment, right now. You know yourself better than anyone.

"If you've never had sex, how can you know for sure?"
There are plenty of things I've never done that I'm sure I wouldn't like. I've never jumped out of an airplane. I've never been punched in the face. I've never had a finger cut off. But I'm pretty sure I wouldn't enjoy any of them.

This microaggression stems from that cultural belief that everyone, as a default, wants to have sex. *All you have to do is try it once*, this microaggression argues, *because sex is something everyone wants, and you just have to have it so you'll realize how much you want it*. This microaggression is subtly asserting that asexuality is a fiction, a misunderstanding you're having about yourself, a simple error you can clear up with a little roll in the hay.

You don't have to have sex to prove your asexuality. Your asexuality is not something you have to "prove" to anyone through any demonstration or action. Choosing not to have sex does not cast doubt on your understanding of yourself as an asexual person.

Despite the powerful cultural messages and interpersonal pressures that surround us every day, it's important to remember that you don't have to have sex in order to live a full, complete life. Sex may be important for many people, but it doesn't have to be important to you.

"So you must hate sex."
Asexual people are often accused of only being asexual because they hate sex.

This microaggression is again rooted in the belief that sex should be a natural part of everyone's life. Not only does everyone want sex, but everyone *loves* sex. We shouldn't just want to do it—we should want to do it *a lot*. When asexual people don't adhere to this construct, sometimes the only answer people can come up with is that we must hate sex.

As we discussed in Chapter 3 this is far from the truth. Sex-favorable asexual people enjoy sex a lot. They seek it out and find a lot of pleasure in it. Sex-neutral ace folks, while not always seeking it out, are content to engage in sex for reasons not associated with sexual attraction. Asexuality is about a person's relationship to sexual attraction only, and there is a wide variety of ways an asexual person can relate to sex. "So you must hate sex," invalidates sex-favorable and sex-neutral ace folks, unfairly questioning the truth of their asexual experience.

But what about sex-averse or sex-repulsed ace folks? Don't they hate sex? Asexual people who choose not to include sex in their lives aren't necessarily sex-hating individuals. They may hate sex for themselves—which is a perfectly valid way to feel about sex in relation to your own body—but it doesn't mean they hate sex for others or in general. Unlike allosexual people who make the assumption that everyone should want and enjoy sex as much as they do, sex-averse and sex-repulsed ace folks are making choices about their own bodies and their own lives, and those choices should not be twisted to place them in some kind of opposition to allosexuality.

Before we move on, it's important to note that the microaggression of "So you must hate sex" isn't exclusive to asexual people. It's an accusation or assumption that, along with its inverse of "So, you must be obsessed with sex," is leveled at many marginalized identities. Race, gender, disability, and other parts of a person's identity and experience can trigger these stereotypes. And the way an individual's different identities intersect can intensify or change how those stereotypes impact them. We'll discuss this concept more in Chapter 10, but for now, just remember: Our culture weaponizes wanting or not wanting sex across many different identities and experiences as a way to marginalize them. It's not exclusive to asexuality.

"You just haven't found the right person."
This microaggression sits at the intersection of two powerful cultural beliefs: the belief that everyone naturally wants sex and the belief that everyone naturally wants a relationship. If you think you're asexual, this reason goes, you must be missing something. And that something may be a person to get your engine running. So get out there, and when you find that person, you'll find your sexual attraction.

Most allosexual people experience—or are taught they should experience—their attractions as connected feelings moving in a single direction. That unity is what they're seeking out all the time. They're looking for "the one," the person who sparks their physical passion, their emotional passion, and their desire to build a permanent bond. But instead of treating this kind of connection as just one of the ways humans can build and experience meaningful relationships, our culture insists that finding "the one" is a universal desire. We *all* want this, in this particular way, and if we don't, there's something wrong with us.

Asexual people (and aromantic people, who we'll learn more about in Chapter 7) confront this idea and question it. Asexuality and aromanticism demonstrate that other options exist, that attractions work independently, that we can build lives without sex or love, that we can form lasting lifelong partnerships that aren't based in this all-consuming idea of "the one."

The right relationship isn't a solution to your asexuality. Your asexuality doesn't require a solution. You can be a complete person as an asexual person without a relationship, and a relationship won't change your reality as an asexual person. The only person you need to rely on to create the life you want to lead is you.

"You just want to feel special."
This microaggression is one of the stranger ones I've encountered in my life.

Asexual people are sometimes accused of only embracing asexuality as a way to be "special," to differentiate themselves from others, to brag about being part of an exclusive club, to look down on others who are "normal."

What a strange thing to think.

There's an idea floating around in our public discourse that marginalized people of all kinds—racial minorities, sexual minorities, gender minorities, disabled people, and the like—are given "special treatment" on the basis of their minority identities. It's believed we're given more than "normal" people are given: more rights, more visibility, more opportunities, more everything. Our existence is seen, by people who hold this belief, as an advantage. We're getting things they aren't.

This view of the world is really misleading. Marginalized people aren't receiving special treatment or advantages. We're either just simply visibly existing in spaces and communities we never did before, or we're being let into opportunities, rights, and spaces that have historically been denied us. We aren't occupying space that belongs to someone else. We're occupying our space that we'd been wrongfully pushed out of before.

For some people, this feels deeply uncomfortable. It feels like something is being taken from them. For people who believe this, making things more fair and equitable for every person feels like a personal attack. And in response, they can attack right back.

Asexuality isn't a "special" identity. In reality, it's allosexuality that's treated as "special." It's what's expected of every person from the moment we're born. It's embedded in an abundance of cultural messages we receive every day. It's centered in the stories we consume, the songs we enjoy on the radio, the ads we see on television, the world we walk through every day. Any deviation from allosexuality is scolded, shunned, pushed aside, made invisible. If anyone in this culture is "special," it's allosexual folks.

Embracing your asexuality and naming your asexuality isn't a grab at specialness. It's a brave step in owning your truth and claiming your space in a world that would rather you didn't.

"All this asexual stuff is just making things more complicated than they really are."

This microaggression dismisses asexuality's intrinsic validity and is rooted in the way dominant cultural ideas render some of the world's complexity invisible.

When people accuse asexual people of just "making things more complicated than they are," they're often referring to the intricate way ace communities think of sex and attraction (the multiple kinds of attraction, the split-attraction model, and the like) and the language that's been developed to fully describe that intricacy (terms like "sex-favorable" and "sex-repulsed," the microlabels, and the like). These things crop up in the mainstream allosexual experience, as well. But while the ace community is parsing out whether a feeling is emotional attraction or alterous attraction, or trying to figure out under what conditions one might be experiencing sexual attraction and in what capacity they're willing to engage in sexual activity, in the allosexual community, you're either attracted or you're not.

This is not to say that allosexual people are having less complicated or less sophisticated experiences of sex and attraction. The opposite is true. They *are* having equally complicated experiences of those things. But because our culture is designed to both encourage and reward the allosexual experience, it doesn't *seem* as complicated. It just seems *normal*, and all of that other stuff—the messy, complex asexual stuff—feels like overdoing it.

Let's look to physics for a way to frame this.

Allosexuality is like experiencing the world through the classical theory of physics. The classical theory of physics describes the way the world works in a way that reflects what we see when we look at the world. We can absorb the rules and ideas of the classical theory of physics and see those things happening in the world around us. The two things line up.

Asexuality is a bit more like quantum physics. Quantum physics describes the way the world works in a way that seems weird and a little counterintuitive. It doesn't describe things we're seeing when we look at the world, and in some cases, it describes things and rules that are diametrically opposed to what we can observe in the world. The two things don't line up.

On the surface, it can feel like the classical theory of physics and quantum physics describe two separate worlds, but they don't. They're describing the *same* world, at radically different scales. They're not in opposition. They're views of the same system from two very different vantage points.

Allosexuality and asexuality exist together in a similar way. They seem to be two separate rulebooks for experiencing sex and attraction. But in fact, they're just two different ways of operating under the same rulebook. All of the complexity we've discussed in this book about asexuality and how asexual people are experiencing sex and attraction is happening for allosexual folks as well. They experience different kinds of attraction. They can have attractions that work independently of each other. They can have varying relationships to the physical act of sex. They can experience change and variation in that experience over the course of their lives.

Allosexual folks just play by the rules in a way that hides the complexity. Asexual folks, on the other hand, play by the rules in a way that reveals and illuminates the complexity. But it's all the same complexity, no matter which road you're taking.

Don't internalize someone's dismissal of your asexuality as "just trying to make it more complicated." You're not trying to create something that isn't there. You just understand things differently.

Microaggressions and aphobia

Throughout this chapter, we've explored a number of asexual microaggressions that can pick away at our confidence and make us question our asexuality. They're all expressions of something larger, a cultural force that works against asexual people: aphobia.

Aphobia (or sometimes acephobia) is the system of discriminatory attitudes, ideas, feelings, and behaviors toward asexuality that inflicts harm or inequitable treatment on asexual people. Discrimination against asexual people—large or small, institutionally or interpersonally, in the culture at large or between you and one other person—is born from aphobia. It's a force we brush up against in the world, and it's a force we struggle against within ourselves.

The consequences of aphobia can be simple, like many of the negative experiences we've explored throughout this chapter. But they can also be dangerously severe: assault, overmedicalization, domestic abuse, and corrective rape. And there's no real way to quantify the long-term damage that aphobia can cause individuals mentally and emotionally throughout their lives as they struggle to both accept their asexuality and live it freely when they do.

If you can recognize the microaggressions we've discussed here and their variants in the world, you can spot aphobia. Be vigilant. Be aware of when aphobic ideas are embedded in the things you're told, the experiences you're having, the demands people make of you, and the thoughts you have about your asexuality.

Aphobia is powerful. But you can be more powerful.

Stick to what you know

This chapter doesn't represent or address every microaggression you might encounter. Unfortunately, it remains easier for some people to find new ways to be cruel than it is for them to find new ways to be compassionate. The microaggressions here are the big ones, and you'll face variations and combinations of these sentiments as you move through your ace experience.

But stick to what you know. Trust yourself and your ability to understand your own experience. Even if you're not one hundred percent sure of all the intricacies and details of how asexuality works for you, don't let someone bombarding you with ideas and stereotypes like these make you lose your faith in yourself.

Chapter 7

ASEXUALITY AND RELATIONSHIPS: CAN I HAVE THEM AND WHAT KIND CAN I HAVE?

Because I create ace education content online, most people know about my aceness before they know anything else about me. Sometimes my aceness is all they know about me.

Every so often, I'll get a message from an allo person who's found my content, thanking me for what I'm doing and sharing that they've learned something. They're generally pleasant interactions: short, to the point, appreciative, kind.

But there was this one message. It came on Instagram from a woman who made it clear she was "definitely not asexual," but she came across my video on Facebook (someone had shared it there) and she found it very interesting.

As I said, I'm not asexual, and I've never thought about what it's like for people to be asexual before. But watching your video made me think about it a little. I didn't know my friend was asexual, and now I understand her better. I'm glad you're doing this for people. I hope one day you find someone who accepts you for what you are. You deserve that.

Sounds sweet, right? Sure. But that last bit—"I hope one day you find someone who accepts you for what you are"—really bugged me. Why did she assume I was single? And why did she assume I'd have to wait for "one day," this far off, distant day in the future, when someone would accept me as an asexual?

Here's what I replied:

> Thank you for the message. I'm glad you got something out of the video your friend shared. The stuff I make is aimed at helping ace folks feel empowered to live their best lives, but it's awesome when allo folks come away feeling the same. And in regard to finding someone one day: I have! Two people, actually. I'm polyamorous, and I have two serious partners. I've been married to my husband, Neil, for the past seven years. And my other partner is Scott, and we've been together for around six months. They're both allo, like you, and they think I'm pretty great. So, "one day" is today, I guess!

I didn't get a response immediately, so I figured our interaction was over. She must have gotten the message that her sentiment annoyed me a little. But a few days later, I heard from my "definitely not asexual" friend again.

> I'm surprised you're married with an additional partner. And I'm surprised neither one of them is like you. Maybe it's wrong on my part, and no offense, but I assumed relationships weren't easy to find for people like you.

I could have written back, lecturing my new "friend" on how *very* offensive her "no offense" comment was, how making the assumption that asexual people can't find relationships is rooted in harmful stereotypes about asexuality, how it shouldn't be a surprise that an allo person wanted to be in a relationship with an ace person, because we're all more than just the sex we might or might not want to have. But I didn't. Getting into a war of passive-aggression in the DMs of my

Instagram account with some allo woman I didn't even know wouldn't achieve anything. She would just think I'm a jerk. And it wouldn't end the negative assumptions the world makes about asexual people and relationships.

The misconceptions and misunderstandings we face as ace people about who we are as individuals branch out and take on new forms when we enter the world of relationships. Those negative messages that twist and contort the way we see ourselves also negatively transform the way we imagine ourselves building connections with other people.

This chapter explores, in a broad manner, how asexuality intersects with relationships. We'll answer some basic questions about relationships that come up for many people when they discover their asexuality. We'll take a look at aromanticism, the orientation including people who do not experience or rarely experience romantic attraction. And we'll look at some of the alternatives to traditional relationships that some asexual folks turn to in order to build the families and human networks they want.

Can asexual people have relationships?

Of course we can!

Asexual people are the focus of a number of negative stereotypes and assumptions, but none bothers me more than the assumption we can't have or don't want relationships. And I'm not just referring to romantic relationships, either. It's often assumed that we don't want or are unable to sustain relationships of *any* kind, as though asexuality hits some off switch on the human capacity to relate and bond with other humans. It's an offensive stereotype, and ultimately it's a nonsensical one—allosexual people do just fine building human connections with people they're not having sex with—but it's one asexual people, especially early in the journey of accepting our identity, can easily internalize.

You can be ace and have romantic relationships. You can be ace and develop powerful friendships. You can be ace and form networks of support and connection of all kinds. Your asexuality does not remove that from your possibilities. Your asexuality doesn't mean you should be alone.

Is it easy? Not really. It's one thing to release internalized aphobia like this and see yourself as an attractive commodity for relationship-building. But other people have to agree, and that's where we hit stumbling blocks. Many people, due to a lack of understanding about asexuality and the lives of asexual people, decide, before even knowing us, that we are not "relationship material." We face more obstacles in building the relationships we want. We just have to approach them a little differently.

How can you have a relationship and not have sex?

Relationships can be formed and be successful without sex.

When we casually say "relationships," most people default to thinking of romantic ones, and we've developed a strong image of what the Perfect Romantic Relationship should be. It looks something like this: two people, deeply in love with each other, desperately attracted to each other, profoundly committed to spending the rest of their lives together with no other person to come between them, and their love burning like a white-hot flame for the rest of their lives.

This idea, while maybe exciting to think about, is in almost every circumstance an unattainable fantasy. It's the composite of several cultural forces—some we've touched on, some we'll get to later—that tie love and sex together and endow that duo with massive social heft and power. It's an idea so powerful that any relationship that deviates from it in any way is the subject of social and cultural scorn.

But the reality of relationships is entirely different. Humans form all manner of relationships to fulfill our needs. Some are romantic. Some are not. Some of those contain love and sex. Some contain only one or the other. Some contain neither and forgo commitment. Some contain neither but embrace commitment. Some focus on a single partner.

Some fulfill separate needs with a multiplicity of partners. Just as there are countless ways to be a human, there are countless ways to connect your life to another human's and form a bond.

If your asexuality doesn't include sex, you can still have relationships if you want them. They may not look like the Perfect Romantic Relationship, but no one's relationship really does. You can build something that works for you.

What if I don't want romantic relationships? Isn't that part of being asexual?

First, it's perfectly fine to not want romantic relationships. There are many people who don't desire them, don't participate in them, and don't include them in the structures of their lives. For some, it's a matter of practicality—being focused on a career, taking time to heal from past emotional wounds, not having the resources to dedicate to romantic pursuit, and the like. For others, it's just a decision to deprioritize romance to focus on growing and evolving themselves.

But some people never feel romantic attraction to anyone. Or they only feel it very rarely, or only in specific circumstances. There's never that moment where they feel, *Wow, I could fall in love with that person*, or *Wow, I really want to do all the romantic things with this person*.

Someone who does not or rarely experiences romantic attraction is called aromantic. Like asexuality, aromanticism describes an experience of the world that does not include or only sometimes includes the experience of one of the attractions. Aromanticism is not a broken form of alloromanticism (experiencing romantic attraction), and aromanticism is a full, complete human experience that is just one of the ways to be in the world.

Aromanticism has its own intricacies, language, and perspective on the world, and a dive into that world would require a book all its own. While this book will not take a deep look at aromanticism, I thought it was important to explore it a little and situate it within our exploration of asexuality.

Are aromanticism and asexuality the same thing?

Aromanticism and asexuality are not the same thing. They are separate experiences, even though they share some similarities.

As you explore aromanticism, you'll find that much of the language and many of the ideas resonate with and resemble words and ideas in asexuality. The two communities share commonalities and there are overlaps in the populations that inhabit each community, but it's important to remember they are distinct and separate things.

Asexuality is concerned with an individual's experience of *sexual* attraction.

Aromanticism is concerned with an individual's experience of *romantic* attraction.

As we learned when we discussed the split-attraction model, these attractions, while they often work together, operate independently, and can be experienced in independent ways.

Can you be asexual and aromantic?

Yes. An individual can be both asexual and aromantic.

Just like most people experience both sexual and romantic attraction in the same direction, there are people who don't experience either sexual or romantic attraction. They inhabit a place under both umbrellas. They're aromantic asexuals, or aro-ace for short.

Aro-ace can include anyone who finds themselves situated in some part of the ace and aro experience. So you can be strictly asexual and aromantic. Or you could be a demisexual aromantic. Or an asexual grayromantic. Aro-ace encompasses all of them.

Do you have to be both?

Asexuality and aromanticism do not have to be experienced together. They absolutely can be, but it's not a requirement.

You can be asexual and still be alloromantic (experiencing romantic attraction).

You can be aromantic and still be allosexual.

The idea that asexuality and aromanticism have to be experienced together is a byproduct of the cultural misconception that not experiencing one kind of attraction means you can't experience any of the others. You aren't cut off from all the attractions just because you're not experiencing one.

If I'm aromantic or aro-ace, are relationships possible?

Absolutely.

Being aromantic or aro-ace doesn't mean you can't pursue or develop relationships. There are many different kinds of relationship structures (which we'll explore a little later in this chapter) that aromantic and aro-ace folks can find themselves in. Some contain elements of romance, and some do not. But all of them can be negotiated and evolve into thriving relationships for aromantic and aro-ace folks.

When should I tell someone I'm interested in I'm asexual?

The question of disclosure is a tricky one.

You're under no obligation—without exception—to disclose your asexuality to anyone. You're always the one steering the ship, so this bit of personal information (along with all the other bits of personal information you've got) is yours until you decide to share it.

So, when should you share your asexuality with a prospective dating partner? It depends on the person and the evolving relationship. I don't think putting arbitrary rules around things like this is ever helpful. Each potential relationship is different. When you feel comfortable sharing and when you feel it's important to share is when it's the right time. If there's any "line in the sand" worth considering here, perhaps it's when the relationship is reaching intimacy negotiations. It will be important to clearly express your needs and boundaries, and how your asexuality expresses itself through physical intimacy will be important to bring to the table. But in all situations, it's up to you when and how you disclose.

"But you should have said that up front so I knew not to waste my time!"

As ace folks, we hear this a lot, and no matter how confident and secure we are in ourselves as asexual people, it hurts very deeply to hear.

It stems from a few faulty premises.

First, it stems from the belief that experiencing sexual attraction is a default human experience and that asexuality is an error of sexuality, an absence of it, a broken version of sexuality. The assumption is that everyone braving the dating scene will want sex in a conventional way, and when ace folks upend that assumption, we can be seen as dishonest, withholding, manipulative.

Our existence isn't any of those things. Our asexuality may surprise a potential partner, but it's never a deception. Anyone who asserts that they're owed your disclosure is also working from the assumption that they're also owed your sexuality. And you owe no one either of those things. They're yours to share with someone when you see fit.

This is also rooted in an idea that relationships, in order to be valuable, must move in certain predetermined ways. This includes the idea that a relationship must at some point include sex in order to be worth pursuing. This is part of an idea called compulsory sexuality, which we'll explore more in Chapter 10. Compulsory sexuality is the cultural belief that wanting to have sex (in particular, the socially approved kind) is an essential, universal part of the human experience. This idea is embedded in the way we think about relationships and their value. If we love someone, this cultural norm insists, then we will not only bond with them emotionally. We'll desire to bond with them physically. And as long as those emotional bonds are present, the desire for those physical bonds will also persist. Without that desire for sex and sexual bonding, the relationship is faulty, false, or basically a dead end.

This way of thinking limits the kind of relationships people believe are worth pursuing, so the fact of our asexuality, as well as the misconceptions people bring to the table, makes many believe that we're a "waste of time." If relationships without sex are inferior relationships, then people who don't want sex are inferior partner possibilities. And *asexuals should know this*, this line of thinking goes, so it's their responsibility to put the damage on the table up front. So an unsuspecting allo won't be caught unaware.

Being a sexual person isn't a universal price of admission for a relationship. Your asexuality and whether or not you want to make sex a part of your relationship doesn't automatically discount you as a possible partner. Don't let this cultural pressure force you into disclosing in a space and time that don't work for you. The assertions and assumptions of compulsory sexuality are not things we need to internalize. We don't have to play by its rules.

It's a feature, not a bug

I remember sitting in my therapist's office, eyes focused down on my two hands clenched into fists, not being able to even fathom making eye contact, speaking in something just above a mumble.

"The thing I can't figure out...*how* am I going to do this? How is anyone going to love me? How is anyone going to put up with this? Being asexual is just like...one more hurdle I have to—"

"Why do you think it's a hurdle?"

Because what else could it be? my mind thought. I sat there, thinking it through.

My therapist gave me some silence to process. Then, very gently:

"What if it's not a hurdle to overcome? What if it's just a fact of yourself? One of many facts that are true of who you are."

"But it's a fact of me that makes me broken, and—"

"Who says it makes you broken?"

"*Everyone.* My entire life, people have told me I'm not quite good enough. Partners have told me I'm not a good enough lover for them, and they find someone else. I try to make friends with gay guys, but they don't get me, because I don't think about or care about sex the same way they do. I've always felt like there was something different about me—more different than just being gay—that kept me cut off from most people, and now I know what it is. But knowing what it is doesn't make it less of a liability."

"Do you think they treat your asexuality that way because they see that *you* treat it that way, and they feel as though they have permission to do so as well?"

My breath caught in my throat. *Oh man,* I thought. *I never looked at it that way before.* Sure, I'd experienced plenty of negative responses to my asexuality, even before I knew what it was. I'd felt a lot of shame and rejection because of it. There were messages coming from everywhere around me, telling me that how I was experiencing the world was a problem.

But I was also relaying those messages to myself. The calls were coming from inside the house, as well. And for every negative message I was getting from someone "out there," I was reinforcing and affirming it with a negative message of my own, too.

That shift in thinking was instrumental in my journey not only to love myself as an asexual person but to develop stronger relationships with my partners. How you treat your asexuality sets expectations for the way prospective partners will treat it. They're taking cues from *you*, and what you project, they'll likely reflect. If you treat your asexuality as a problem or an obstacle, they'll probably do the same. If you treat your asexuality as something worthy of respect, you stand a better chance of getting that in return.

So treat your asexuality as a feature, not a bug.

So often in the relationship game, we apologize for our asexuality. We present it to our prospective partners as "something they'll have to get used to," or "something they'll have to learn to accept." We place our asexuality on the relationship table as an issue that will require resolving, a puzzle that requires solving. That's a self-fulfilling prophecy. We tell our partners that "asexuality is a problem!" and it becomes one.

But we don't have anything to apologize for. We aren't a puzzle or an issue or a problem. Our asexuality is just a part of who we are, one facet of our complete story, and anyone who enters into a relationship with us should see it as a cool feature of us, not some bug in the system that needs repair.

Will there be work to do? Sure. Without question. You'll have to negotiate with your partner how your asexuality intersects and interacts with their sexual identity. But this negotiation isn't unique to asexuality. *Everyone* goes through this. Every relationship requires this work. The challenges you and your prospective partners will face are grounded in the challenges of *relationships*, not of asexuality.

Relationships are hard. Asexuality isn't.

Treat your own asexuality the way you want a partner to treat it. Lead by example.

What kind of relationship can I have?

There is no kind of relationship that's inherently off limits to you simply because you're asexual.

There are no "buts" here. No disclaimers. It's as straightforward as that.

Asexuality doesn't limit the kinds of relationships you can seek out or aspire to have. You may be limited by the people you encounter and engage with as prospective partners—we can't control how others construct or pursue relationship partners—but asexuality doesn't take any kind of relationship off the table as a default. Asexuality doesn't remove your options.

It's important to recognize it won't always *feel* this way. Asexual folks often experience a lot of rejection in the relationship game and endure a lot of aphobia while seeking out partners. As those negative experiences build up, it can feel like asexuality is the root cause of struggle. It can feel like your aceness is standing in between you and a relationship.

It's aphobia that stands in the way. It's prospective partners that hold misguided ideas about us that stand in the way. It's partners who are unwilling to explore, unwilling to think outside of the bounds a little, unwilling to expand and negotiate their relationship expectations that stand in the way. But your asexuality is not the obstacle.

Any relationship structure you want to pursue that feels right to you and that provides you with the kind of security, support, and community you want is possible for you to explore. You have a right to ask for it. You have a right to build it with a willing partner. You have a right to shape your life around it.

The following sections detail some of the main relationship structures that are available for exploration. These sections don't explain them in great detail—each relationship structure could be the subject of their own book—and they aren't meant to be the definitive word on the subject.

The information here gives you a glimpse of what's possible and offers you a starting point for thinking about the kind of relationship you might want to pursue.

Monogamy
Monogamy is the most common relationship structure out there, and the one you're likely most familiar with. It describes a relationship between two people that's exclusive both sexually and emotionally. In a monogamous relationship, both partners consent to being the only other partner for the other person. There are no other romantic or emotional relationships formed. There are no other sexual relationships formed.

A casual glance at the world around us, in both the real world of other people and the imagined world of our consumable media, shows us how dominant monogamy is as a relationship structure. It's so dominant that many people consider it the default human relationship and believe that it's within our nature to seek out and thrive in monogamous relationships.

This isn't the case. Not only are there other relationship structures that we can seek out and thrive in, but monogamy, despite its prevalence, can be a struggle for many people. Monogamy is just one of the ways we can build our human networks, and there is no particular moral or intrinsic good in monogamy that isn't present in other relationship structures. This is not to say that monogamy, in and of itself, is bad. It's not. Many people form lifelong, happy, and successful monogamous relationships that provide them with fulfillment and security. But the toxic culture we build around monogamy, a culture that exerts powerful pressure on *everyone* to pursue and fit a monogamous mold, can negatively impact people who just aren't built for it.

You can be interested in monogamy with or without sex. Monogamy, like all other relationship structures, does not require sex. The only requirement of monogamy is exclusivity. How you achieve and practice that exclusivity is up to you and your monogamous partner. You can pursue monogamy with a partner even if you don't want to include sex or other forms of intense intimacy in your relationship. If a partner tells you, "Well, if we're going to be monogamous, you have to be willing to…," they're projecting their wants and not reflecting what's true. Monogamy only works when both partners agree to the terms of the exclusive commitment. If both partners agree to exclusivity without sexual activity, you're set.

Monogamy doesn't fix your fears. Sometimes, people choose relationship structures to address other fears or concerns they have as individuals. People can choose monogamy as a way to limit the things they're afraid of—losing the relationship, their partner finding someone they like and care for more, their partner being unfaithful— and believe it's the way to ensure that those fears never become a reality. No relationship structure can do that for you. Your fears, insecurities, and anxieties will be there, regardless of the relationship structure you choose. If you're looking at monogamy because you think it'll fix your fears, you're looking at monogamy for the wrong reasons. Choose it because it's the kind of relationship you thrive in, the kind of relationship that allows you to be the full human being you are, not because it's the one that'll keep your terrors at bay.

Consensual non-monogamy

Sometimes, because of their personal needs and desires, individuals will choose to build relationships where exclusive commitment—both romantic and/or sexual—is not required. This kind of relationship, where the people involved may have multiple emotional or sexual partners or a combination of both, is called consensual non-monogamy.

Consensual non-monogamy relies on open and honest communication where all partners consent to an agreed-upon set of rules to work. It's built on trust, care, and mutual respect. Consensual non-monogamy does not represent a lesser or more diminished form of commitment than monogamy, despite what dominant cultural messages might tell you. Consensual non-monogamous partners can form deep and lasting lifelong commitments, and their support and care for each other can be as deep as those in exclusively monogamous relationships. For consensually non-monogamous couples, it's okay for there to be other important and valued kinds of connections with people, and those connections can exist within and alongside the others.

Consensual non-monogamy can take different forms, depending on the needs and desires of the people involved. Sometimes, the agreement of a consensually non-monogamous relationship will allow only outside sexual connections while maintaining the exclusivity of the emotional relationship. Sometimes, connections of all kinds are allowed. What's important is that all agreements are consented to by all parties in the relationship, and that honest communication about evolving connections takes place.

Consensual non-monogamy isn't an excuse for cheating. One of the most important parts of consensual non-monogamy is the "consensual" part. Consent, the clear, freely given agreement between individuals to mutually engage in something, is necessary and foundational here. Engaging in activities that aren't part of your agreement or developing new connections without the knowledge of your partner or partners is not consensual non-monogamy. Everyone's consent is required. Everyone's knowledge is required. Everyone's honesty is required. Cheating and dishonesty aren't given a free pass just because you're practicing consensual non-monogamy.

Consensual non-monogamy isn't required because you're asexual. I've encountered many ace folks who believe or are led to believe by potential partners that a non-monogamous relationship is the only kind of relationship ace folks can reasonably expect, usually a message sent by allosexual folks. Consensual non-monogamy is an option, not an imperative. Relationships should not be designed around the sexual needs of one partner, and no one partner's needs should dictate the choices of the other. You can work together to choose the relationship structure that works for you. You can work together to determine the way your relationship structure will be organized. But no one choice is demanded of you because you're asexual. Choose consensual non-monogamy because it's the structure that leads to the most fulfilling relationships for you.

Open relationships

One form of consensual non-monogamy is open relationships. While open relationships can be classified as any consensually non-monogamous relationship, the term is generally used to describe those consensually non-monogamous relationships that allow multiple sexual partners but demand emotional exclusivity. Open relationships can address the needs and desires of many different kinds of relationships: relationships that have become sexless, relationships with partners having mismatched libidos, relationships where one partner enjoys sexual activities the other partner does not, and relationships where partners choose to explore their sexual horizons with other people together. Open relationships can also be an option for ace/allo relationships with asexual partners who want little or no sex.

Open relationships still require consent. Open relationships are not a code word for permissible cheating. Open relationships are not a free-for-all. Even though they're only focused on sexual non-exclusivity, they still require truthful conversation and mutual partner consent. Everyone involved has to agree on the boundaries around which other sexual partners can be pursued. "Open" doesn't mean "unbounded."

For ace/allo couples, "open" doesn't just have to apply to the allo partner. Ace people in open relationships can have multiple sexual partners, too. Often, we assume that if an ace/allo couple is pursuing an open relationship, it's for the benefit of the allo partner while the ace partner remains monogamous. This isn't necessarily so. Any partner in an open relationship, if they so desire, should be free to pursue additional connections. Despite the way we view asexuality culturally, relationships do not have to be designed around the needs of an allo partner. Allosexuality isn't supreme. If a partner tells you, "We can be open, but *you* have to be monogamous because you're the ace one," they're constructing a relationship dynamic that's unfair. A partner in an open relationship can choose not to pursue other connections, but it should not be required of them, especially if it's because they're ace.

Polyamory
Polyamory is a form of consensual non-monogamy that's most commonly understood as a relationship structure that encourages and supports individuals having multiple emotional and romantic relationships. In polyamory, you can be in love with multiple people, you can date multiple people, and you can pursue long-term relationships with multiple people. In polyamory, these relationships can be kept separate, or they can be intertwined. They can be ordered in a hierarchy of importance ("This is my primary partner, and this is my secondary partner"), or they can exist without hierarchy, each

relationship being as important as another. Polyamorous relationships can contain connections of varying seriousness, commitment, and longevity. What connects all the options in polyamory is a belief that one connection doesn't diminish another, and people can experience fulfilling, meaningful relationships without exclusivity.

Polyamory is the relationship structure I choose for myself. My husband and I each have another partner. And the four of us are all connected through friendship. This kind of polyamorous unit is called a polycule. Since my partner, Scott, is an astrophysicist, we began calling our polycule "the constellation." Each relationship in our constellation, regardless of its nature, matters, and everyone in the constellation works to support each relationship. While many people in the world might look down on the way we've structured our lives, the members of my constellation show up every day with care, affection, empathy, and kindness for every other member, and our family works hard to make everyone feel loved.

Polyamory is not a free-for-all. One of the common misconceptions about polyamory is that it's a total free-for-all. Everyone involved gets to do whatever they want, whenever they want, with whoever they want. It's perceived to be a kind of relationship chaos that lacks the maturity and stability of monogamous relationships. While polyamory can be practiced in ways that free its participants to enjoy many different relationships at once, it's not a chaos that leaves people's feelings and safety unconsidered. Remember: It's a form of consensual non-monogamy, which requires the open and honest communication of everyone involved and everyone's consent for what bonds are being developed. Unconsidered, uncaring, and unconsenting relationship building is *not* polyamory.

Polyamory doesn't fix everything. In the same way that monogamy doesn't fix your fears, insecurities, and anxieties by limiting what's possible, polyamory doesn't provide quick fixes by expanding options. It can be seductive to think of polyamory as an easy way to avoid the bumps and bruises of negotiating a relationship through the way you experience asexuality. *If my partner doesn't have to get everything from me*, you may think, *then that's going to solve everything, right?* You can't structure your way out of working through your own baggage. A relationship structure can't process your issues. Choose polyamory because it's something you want and it's something that allows you space to be the best version of yourself. Don't choose it as an escape hatch from your asexuality. You'll be setting yourself and your partners up for disappointment.

Queerplatonic relationships

Not all relationship structures include romantic and sexual connections.

Queerplatonic relationships (sometimes QPRs for short) are relationships that blur the lines between romantic and platonic relationships. QPRs are relationships that push past the expected boundaries and norms of platonic relationships but don't become confined within the boundaries and norms of romantic relationships. Queerplatonic relationships reject the expectations that a serious, foundational relationship must include sex or romance. They are relationships outside of those constructs, and outside the usual expectations society has for people in relationships.

Queerplatonic relationships evolved as an idea in the aromantic and asexual communities, responding to the unique ways aromantic and asexual people build and value connections. QPRs provide a relationship structure that acknowledges aromanticism and asexuality as full human experiences, not as experiences that have to fit themselves into more expected sexual and romantic boxes. For many aromantic and asexual folks, queerplatonic relationships provide a structure that reflects the way they experience the world.

Can a QPR contain sex or romantic things? This is a common question surrounding queerplatonic relationships. Yes, a QPR can contain sex. Yes, a QPR can contain romantic gestures or romantic elements. These activities are decided upon and mutually consented to by the people involved. But what makes a relationship of this kind a QPR is how the people involved define and articulate their feelings.

Remember, queerplatonic relationships push and bend the boundaries of platonic and romantic relationships.

But QPRs aren't "real" relationships, right? Queerplatonic relationships are every bit as real as any monogamous or ethically non-monogamous relationship. Their existence outside of the sexual and romantic norms of relationships doesn't mean they lack substance or seriousness. People in QPRs build long-term, lifelong, committed relationships that provide all the security, support, and care of any other relationship structure. QPRs are real relationships. They're real to the people in them, and whether or not they're understood, they should be respected.

Okay, but QPRs are just really good friendships, right? No. Queerplatonic relationships are not "just friendships." The absence of sex and/or romance in a relationship does not automatically classify it as a friendship. Sex does not bestow a deeper importance on a relationship. Romance does not bestow a deeper importance on a relationship. A relationship can become something other than friendship in ways that don't include sex or romance. To dismiss queerplatonic relationships as "just friendships" not only diminishes the experience of the people in the QPR, but it also betrays an unfair devaluation of friendships as well.

Friendships

I don't think we talk enough about friendships.

So often in our cultural conversations about relationships (and in the one we've had in a good bit of this chapter so far) we assume "relationship" implies romantic relationships. We don't include friendships in the way we think and talk about relationships, as though they are a different species of relationship that doesn't and can't sit alongside romantic ones.

We look at friendships as something we graduate from, into the more "real" romantic relationships. We consider friendships not as serious or substantial as romantic relationships. We assume people will choose their romantic partners over their friends without question. We see friendships as less important, less valuable, less "real."

This does a great disservice to friendships, because friendships can be some of the most powerful and transformative relationships of our lives. Well-cared for, respected, and nurtured platonic friendships can provide just as substantial, just as valuable, and just as sustaining connection as any romantic relationship. Friendships aren't stepping stones to real relationships. Friendships aren't testing grounds for real connections. Friendships can be full and complete relationships on equal footing with any other kind of relationship.

As you explore your identity and its intersection with relationship building, remember that platonic friendships aren't separate from the range of possibilities. They're an important part of the menu.

This is all great. But I'm never *really* going to have a relationship if I'm ace, right?

I wish I could say, "Hey, friends. Don't worry about it! Finding a relationship will be a piece of cake. There are a *billion* people out there who'll be patient and understanding and open-minded and kind. You'll be in the perfect relationship in no time at all!"

I can't. Relationships are hard for asexual people. It's hard to find people who really understand asexuality. It's hard to find allo folks who don't think sex is essential to a relationship. It's hard to find someone who, even if they do agree to deprioritize or remove sex from the menu in a relationship, is willing to treat that relationship seriously in the long-term. It's hard to navigate relationships while ace.

But it's not *impossible*.

I am very happily polyamorous with three allosexual men: my husband, Neil; his partner, Dan; and my partner, Scott.

I met and married Neil before I knew I was ace, and he's stood by me and supported me through my self-realization and coming-out process, one of the hardest parts of my adult life. We built a relationship for several years and had to rewrite the rules when I discovered I was ace. That rewriting was *hard*. We struggled with some very complicated emotions, and even though we are now years into that journey, we still work together to overcome obstacles when they arise, and we renegotiate the rules of our relationships as we evolve as people. But we're *together*. Neil loves me as the asexual man I am. And I love him in return.

Scott and I have been together a much shorter time, but our relationship was built once I knew and understood my aceness. I am the first asexual person Scott's ever dated, and although he is not ace, he treats my asexuality not as a roadblock but as one of the unique things about me that he loves. I show up as myself, and I'm loved as myself. Together, we find ways to honor both of our experiences, lifting each other up and working together when we hit a snag.

I am not in a romantic or sexual relationship with Dan, but I consider him as much a part of my family as Neil and Scott. Dan makes Neil very happy, and he brings a humor and joy to our constellation that we all appreciate deeply. Our relationship isn't romantic or sexual, but Dan and I are still *in relationship* with each other, talking about our collective futures, making plans, providing emotional support, being there for each other.

Ace or allo, romantic relationship or not, monogamy or polyamory, we all should feel empowered to build the network of human connections that spark our hearts and minds. Your asexuality doesn't remove that ability from you.

Find your people. Build your families. Chase the love you want, no matter what it looks like.

Chapter 8

ASEXUALITY AND RELATIONSHIPS: NEGOTIATING INTIMACY WITH YOUR PARTNER

My husband, Neil, and I never had a wedding.

We got married four days after we moved to Connecticut. We headed to downtown Hartford, got our marriage license, and called the first justice of the peace we could find through a Google search, a seemingly nice woman in her sixties named Carol. Since we were so new to Connecticut, Carol was the one who picked out where we got married, the beautiful Rose Garden in Hartford's Elizabeth Park, because we hadn't been there long enough to know anywhere appropriate.

Carol met us at the Rose Garden on a Monday morning, very early. No one was in the park. It was much too early for that. And it was September, so the roses weren't really in bloom, but the greenery that lined the walkways and covered the gazebo in the garden's center were still green. It was beautiful, even if less rose-y than we'd hoped. We walked with Carol to the gazebo and stood with her in the center.

"Ready to go?" she said.

Carol married us in just under ten minutes. She was all business, if a little scattered. She had our ceremony written out longhand on a legal pad, and she kept flipping through the pages, trying to find her place.

It was a little windy, too, so sometimes the pad erupted in chaos, and Carol would fluster to contain the pages flicking this way and that. But we got through it, exchanged our personally written vows, said the "I dos," and were proclaimed married by Carol. Once it was done, Carol wandered back to wherever she had come from, and my husband and I were alone in the quiet of the garden, having woken up single but now very, very *married*.

"So...what do you wanna do now?" my husband asked. That question that had plagued me with fear and anxiety from boyfriends in my twenties didn't fill me with dread here. Thank goodness for growth.

"I'm kinda hungry. Want to grab some food?"

So we found a nearby brunch place, again thanks to Google: The First and Last Cafe, which felt appropriately named. And we had a delightful brunch.

We had no idea what was waiting in front of us. Two grueling years of grad school for him. Plays of mine premiering in New York, New Jersey, and across the ocean in the UK. Our dog, Ophelia. Working our butts off on our respective art in order to feed our souls. Taking taxing jobs in arts administration for both of us in order to pay the bills. Awesome date nights. Awesomely bad fights. Monogamy that turned into polyamory. The dawning of my asexuality. Two new partners. New career goals. And the constant negotiation and compassion that makes all of these changes bearable.

We've now been married for almost eight years, and as much as I sometimes wish we would have had a big drawn-out wedding with lots of people and food and music and celebration, I'm glad our commitment to each other was so specifically *ours*. Because, while our marriage does rely on the support of everyone around us, in the end, it's only up to us to make the thing succeed. He creates space for me to be me. I create space for him to be him. And through all the accommodations and adjustments and compromises and collaborations, we create a space that's more an *us*. No one else can do that for us.

Because there's no one else in the garden. Not even Carol.

The same is true for your relationship. It's up to you to make it work. And this chapter will explore how to negotiate one particular corner of your relationship: intimacy. Intimacy can be one of the most challenging areas for relationships, and for ace folks, this area can be exponentially more daunting.

So we'll look at the foundational work you and your partner should do to get the ball rolling around intimacy. And we'll check out ways to negotiate physical intimacy within your relationship.

A disclaimer: This chapter is mostly looking at relationships through a few specific lenses. It's considering relationships that likely contain romantic and/or sexual components. It's also considering relationships that are likely inhabited by an ace person involved with an allo person. If these aren't the kinds of relationships you're involved in or interested in pursuing, this chapter might not hold much for you. That's okay! You can skip ahead. You don't have to be in these kinds of relationships to be ace.

But through my work as an educator, I've encountered so many ace folks struggling with navigating these kinds of relationships. I wanted to make sure this book included a section that spoke to their struggles—struggled I've known myself—and offered some ideas on addressing them.

Know and define your boundaries

If there's a key thing that makes a relationship work, it's boundaries. Defining and discussing your boundaries with your partner, whether you're ace or allo, creates the space for you to safely explore what it is the two of you are together.

Let's start with defining your boundaries.

Think about boundaries as a set of rules, guidelines, and limits that define two things: what we will and won't do, and what's permissible or not for someone else to do. Boundaries aren't only for physical intimacy. We create boundaries in all corners of our relationships. What unifies our boundaries is how they define where you end and the other person begins. Boundaries preserve our personal autonomy, physically, mentally, and emotionally.

The first step to knowing your boundaries around intimacy as an ace person is figuring out how your own asexuality works. Asexuality works differently for each ace person. Some of us have sex, some don't. Some enjoy intimacy, some don't. Some have high libido, some have low libido. Some sex-favorable folks are down for anything. Some aren't. Kink is good for some. For others—not so much. There's no universal asexual experience.

So defining how asexuality works for you is important to understanding your boundaries. Not only will it help you communicate to others, in clear and certain terms, what your body and mind are open to, it will help you feel a sense of control over those things. You will feel safer asking for what you want, rejecting what you don't, and navigating a space to explore new things if you're very clear on the machinery of your asexuality.

Now, it's time to map out your boundaries. Map out what you're comfortable with, what you enjoy, what you're okay with, and what you're not. Be thorough. Be specific. The clearer you are about your boundaries, the more useful they'll be to you.

Questions to help you map out your boundaries

Here are four important questions to get you started thinking through your boundaries and mapping them out:

Am I sex-repulsed, sex-averse, sex-neutral, or sex-favorable? Starting with this basic language helps a lot. Your relationship to sexual activity is going to be something a potential partner will want to know, so having this language to describe it will be a great tool in setting expectations.

If I'm open to sex, what kinds of sexual activities am I comfortable with or do I enjoy? Just knowing you're open to sex still leaves lots of things open-ended and unclear. If you want to craft strong boundaries, you have to know what kinds of activities are part of that openness you have to sex. This can be a little uncomfortable to think about or talk about, and sometimes the answers aren't always clear or can change over time. But the more confidently straightforward you can be about this, the stronger you'll be in negotiating a relationship that works.

What non-sexual forms of intimacy am I comfortable with or do I enjoy? We often forget that sex isn't the only form of intimacy there is. So, when you're thinking through your boundaries, think outside of sex! There are many ways for us to share intimate space with the people we're in relationships with. Think through all the non-sexual ways you enjoy closeness, if you do. Including those in any discussion with a partner around your relationship rules will be very helpful.

What are my dealbreakers? What are my hard "No"s? Some things are going to be off the table, no matter who you're in a relationship with. Give yourself permission to be honest about those things, even if they're things that most "typical" relationships include. If something is a hard "no" for you, be confident enough to articulate it. You don't have to compromise and acquiesce to anyone. Your dealbreakers are an important part of building a relationship that works for you. Don't ignore them. Don't sell them short.

These aren't comprehensive questions, but they can get you started thinking about your boundaries. It's important to be specific. Defining your boundaries as clearly and completely as you can will empower you when you're shaping the ground rules of your relationship.

Discussing your boundaries with your partner

Nobody likes uncomfortable conversations, particularly uncomfortable conversations about sex and intimacy. But this conversation—the one where you explain your boundaries to your partner—is so incredibly important to have.

Remember: There is no universal asexual experience. There's also next to zero asexual representation in popular culture. And, on top of that, the asexual representation we have isn't really digging into the secret sex lives of aces. So your partner, no matter how well-meaning and empathetic, may be coming into your relationship with some misconceptions about how asexuality works and how varied the ace experience of sex can be.

Therefore this conversation where you explain your boundaries does double duty. It maps out what a healthy, satisfying, and consensual sex life is to you, and it ensures your partner isn't bringing any aphobic baggage to the relationship table accidentally.

When the time is right—and that's probably early on in a relationship, before things are getting physical but after you've developed a level of trust and comfort with someone—sit down and have the conversation. Explain to your partner what you've mapped out for yourself about your boundaries. Be clear. Be confident. And share them lovingly.

Here are some boundaries discussion DOs:
- DO be honest, straightforward, and complete in your explanation.
- DO communicate your boundaries confidently and kindly.
- DO frame the conversation as a space for collaboration. You're not sitting down to lecture to each other. You're building a stronger relationship *together*.
- DO allow for some questions from your partner, because some of what you explain may be confusing.
- DO reinforce the idea that this is what a healthy, satisfying, and consensual sex life looks like to you.

Here are some DON'Ts:
- DON'T make it a list of demands. Strident language isn't your friend here. Relationships are collaborative things. So framing your boundaries as a list of demands might get in your way.

- DON'T apologize for your boundaries. Your boundaries are yours. And you have nothing to apologize for.
- DON'T backtrack on your boundaries to keep things from getting complicated.
- DON'T be the only person sharing your boundaries, especially if your partner is allo. No one's boundaries should be assumed. So if you're sharing yours, they need to share theirs, ideally as completely and thoughtfully as yours. Help them out, if you need to.

This conversation can get hard. It can get really uncomfortable. And sometimes, it can lead to an impasse in your relationship. But don't automatically assume it means you have to give up on your boundaries or the authentic way you want to live your life. Your asexuality is not automatically subordinate to the sexual wants and needs of your partner. You are not inherently assumed to be second place. So lean into the discomfort if it arises in this conversation. The discomfort now will either help you develop a stronger relationship later or it will tell you that you both need to find something somewhere else.

Boundaries aren't permanent

The boundaries you set today aren't set in stone. Just like your ace identity can be fluid, so can your boundaries around sex and physical intimacy. You will grow and change over time. And each relationship you have will be different. The DNA of your connection to another person isn't a universal constant, so it's okay for your boundaries to shift as you move through your life and as you move from relationship to relationship.

It doesn't make you a hypocrite. It doesn't make your asexuality invalid or inauthentic. It's a natural process of growing and changing. It's totally okay.

So check in with yourself and with your partner every now and then. Maybe you're open to more forms of intimacy. Maybe you'd like to take something off the table. Maybe you just want to re-establish the ground rules around a few things. When you feel like the boundaries need some updating—update them. Renegotiate the contract, so to speak. This is the mark of a healthy relationship and the mark of a healthy relationship with your own asexuality.

Negotiating intimacy

One of the hardest things for me after coming out as asexual was negotiating intimacy. I'm somewhere between sex-neutral and sex-favorable, so this was a real juggling act: navigating my shifting relationship with intimate activities while trying to balance my desire to make sure my allo husband was happy with my own needs as an ace person.

For a long time I didn't really succeed. There were big communication problems. I'd get overwhelmed and pull away from intimacy entirely. We'd have intimacy sometimes that was awkward and unfulfilling. It was just a mess.

It was a mess because we were trying to navigate this new landscape of intimacy for us without any tools, any strategies. We were just flying by the seat of our pants. And that was not a great idea.

With some work, however, we developed some skills and strategies that helped us negotiate intimacy in a way that balanced all of those needs and allowed both of us to have healthy, satisfying, and consensual sex lives. It's always a work in progress, but we have some shape to it now. And that's made a huge difference.

Expand the menu

For most couples, sex is a pretty straightforward concept. The menu is pretty standard. I'm not going to go into details, because I really don't have to. Regardless of your sexual orientation, the dominant cultural narrative of what a "good sex life" is is deeply ingrained in us.

So when you're asexual, the "good sex life" that all of us are being told we need to have in order to be happy isn't a given. Some of us want none of it. Some of us are just generally disinterested in it. Some of us don't mind it, but maybe there are parts and pieces that make us uncomfortable. Whatever your asexual relationship to sex, that "good sex life"—where you're craving your partner, and you're doing it regularly, and you're enjoying the hell out of it—can be the source of a lot of shame and anger and confusion. It can make us pummel ourselves with negative self-talk. It can drown us in inadequacy.

So the first thing we can do as asexual people to regain our control and reassert ourselves is to simply expand the menu. Toss out those cultural expectations and demands about what a "good sex life" is and rewrite them to suit us.

The first step is doing that for ourselves. Asking ourselves, "What does satisfying intimacy look like to me?" And we don't answer that question by holding ourselves up to an allosexual standard and note where we match up and where we're missing. We start from scratch, and really define it *for us*.

If it's just holding hands and cuddling sometimes...then that's a satisfying sex life.

If it's no sexual contact but a hell of a lot of BDSM...then that's a satisfying sex life.

If it's no physical intimacy but a lot of emotional intimacy...then that's a satisfying sex life.

If it's any combination of anything across the intimacy spectrum... then that's a satisfying sex life.

Part of what's awesome about embracing your asexuality is the permission to reject dominant cultural norms. You take the first step when you say, "I'm ace." You reject norms when you say, "I'm ace." Once you take that leap, the next one is easy. You can reject what a "good sex life" is and redefine it for yourself. You can toss out the old menu and write your own.

Share the expanded menu with your partner
So this can be a tough conversation.

We (and I'm talking of that general "we," the everybody "we") have a weird cultural relationship to sex. On the one hand, we are culturally obsessed with it. On the other, we think it's shameful and taboo to talk about it openly and straightforwardly. So this whiplash-inducing hypocrisy around sex makes talking about sex with a partner, ace or allo, really difficult. The difficulty is compounded for ace folks, because we're also upending some general assumptions about how "normal" folks participate in sex and intimacy. And that means this conversation can feel really overwhelming and scary.

When I'm approaching the subject of intimacy with a new partner, I start by framing the conversation positively: "Hey. I'm into you. And I feel like we're getting to the point where intimacy is going to come up. You know I'm ace, so I think it's time we talk about what a healthy, satisfying, consensual sex life looks like for me. And you can tell me about what that looks like for you. And we can see where we go from there."

Notice there's no apologizing. There's no framing my asexuality as a disadvantage or an obstacle. That's important. *You deserve that.* What you want as an ace person, whether you're sex-favorable or sex-repulsed, is valid and, more importantly, *yours.* You don't have to apologize for who you are and what you want.

Then, we get into mechanics. A helpful framework for talking to your partner about your expanded menu is breaking down your menu into three sections: Column Yes, Column No, and Column Maybe.

Column Yes would contain those forms of intimacy that are welcome, that you enjoy. This is the intimacy you seek out, that you're cool initiating, that you find satisfying. Don't just think of this as sex, either. It's all intimacy that's welcome. This is the intimacy you can be fully present for, that can receive your freely given consent. And remember: Even things in this column require your consent in the moment, instance by instance.

Column No would contain those forms of intimacy that are off the table for you. The dealbreakers. This is the intimacy you're drawing clear lines around, that you experience negatively. You won't initiate these, you won't seek them out. You cannot be fully present for these activities. They're the things that cause harm or just the things you don't want to do (both reasons are valid). These activities are the things you do not give consent for.

Column Maybe would contain those forms of intimacy that are up for negotiation, that are sometimes okay. Or at least you'd be open to considering them. These are the forms of intimacy that aren't a hard no, but they're also not the kind of activities that get freely given consent. This column is also for the activities you don't have an answer for, things you haven't tried but want to, things you've tried but haven't made up your mind on. Anything in the gray area goes into Column Maybe. And it's perfectly fine if *everything* is in Column Maybe.

Presenting your expanded menu this way helps your partner clearly understand your needs, wants, and boundaries. And it organizes your menu in a way that is clear and digestible.

Then, as I said earlier, give your partner a chance to share their menu as well. Ace and allo alike, we've all got three columns on our menus. We should all be encouraged to think about our relationship to physical intimacy this way. Just as asexuality shouldn't be assumed to be an "everything is off the table" experience, allosexuality shouldn't be assumed to be a "everything is on the table" experience. Allowing this space for your partner to share as well makes this conversation more collaborative, and it doesn't frame your asexuality as a list of demands. It also gives your partner a chance to think about their own intimacy menu this way. Maybe they never have before! They might surprise themselves with what they discover.

The conversation is a good foundation for building a mutually satisfying intimate relationship with your partner. With both your menus on the table, you can figure out with your partner what entrees and appetizers you'll be sharing later (*wink wink*).

When the columns are unbalanced
I want to acknowledge that for sex-repulsed folks, sex-averse folks, folks who are unable to engage in physical intimacy, and anyone who

for whatever reason has a limited range of physical intimacy or sexual behaviors that are comfortable to them, this menu framework can still feel daunting. Because it's likely that the columns are going to be really unbalanced.

That's why it's important to really break down those cultural ideas of what a "good sex life" looks like and really create an expanded menu of intimacy. Even intimacy that doesn't directly include physical touch. Just because you're not interested in sexual touch or physical intimacy doesn't mean you can't experience intimacy in other ways. Redefine it for you. Present it that way to your partner. You aren't bound to an experience that's simply more common. Your intimacy—in whatever shape it takes—is valid and worthy.

When the columns are really unbalanced, just be ready to discuss the implications. Unbalanced columns aren't an invitation to backtrack on your needs or apologize for your asexuality. Your partner's needs aren't more important or legitimate than yours. Just talk about it. See what common ground you can find. But you don't have to give up who you are and what you aren't to balance the columns for anyone.

The Sliding SexyTimes Scale

So when I'm with an allo partner, after we've had the convo and we're just going through the motions of our relationship, there are the moments we have to go from the theory to the mechanics. We have to talk about actually doing it.

I used to have a lot of anxiety about it. It would trigger all of my ace insecurities and it would bring up all my memories of negative experiences. I'd just want to run out of the room. And that's not going to feel good for a partner who's just trying to be close to you.

So when it's necessary, my partners and I use something I call the Sliding SexyTimes Scale, a very simple negotiation tool to help guide these moments in a way that ensures everyone feels safe, supported, and able to freely consent. It uses a 1–10 scale to articulate how each partner is feeling about intimacy in the given moment.

So the partner who's wanting to initiate some kind of intimacy that's on the expanded menu says something like, "Hey. I'm in the mood for this thing from Column Yes. I'm at a...7. How about you?"

The other partner can respond, with the 1–10 scale, where they are in terms of desire or consent to engage in that activity. "Okay, so I hear you're at 7. I'm right now at a 3."

This is where the expanded menu can really become useful. Once you know where each other is, if both parties are game, you can discuss what might be possible at that moment.

So I might say, "I'm right now at a 3. But if you don't mind cuddling for a while and making out first without jumping to that thing from Column Yes, I could get to a 5 or 6."

Or they might say, "Okay, you're at a 3? No problem. I respect that and I can go take care of this by myself."

Or you might together agree that the thing from Column Yes can wait for another day, but you're at an 8 for this other thing from Column Yes, and that's what's going to be happening today.

The scale helps you describe exactly where you are to your partner, and where you are willing to get to. It helps you set boundaries in the moment clearly. It helps you define your consent. It's an awesome tool.

When I use it with my partners, I feel like I'm in control of my participation in intimacy. And I also feel as though I fully understand where they are, too. If they're just at 5, I might say, "I'm at a 2 and I don't want to be intimate right now." If they're at an 8 or 9, and I'm feeling open to consenting to intimacy, I might say, "Well I'm at a 3, but here's what I'd feel okay with doing today."

The scale makes each encounter its own thing, without past expectations hovering over it. Everyone's clear. Everyone's on the same page. And when you use the scale regularly, both of you remember that the menu and the columns are all dependent on the moment. It's all dependent on each partner's immediate, current consent. Nothing is a given. Everything requires discussion. Everything requires loving, compassionate cooperation.

It may not feel particularly sexy in the moment, but it makes for better experiences overall.

What if I'm already in a relationship and realize I'm ace? What happens then?

I was married to my husband for three and a half years when I came out as asexual. The person he fell in love with, the person he married, the person he'd negotiated an intimate life with was a person he assumed was allosexual. My coming out changed that. All of a sudden, there was something new in our relationship—*someone* new—and it took some time to adjust.

Coming out as asexual when you're in a relationship with someone allo doesn't mean your relationship has to end. But it does mean you have a little extra work to do in order to make things work.

First, you have to both get on the same page. You and your allo partner should make it a relationship priority to become asexuality experts. Learn as much as you both can about asexuality, and teach your partner as much as you can about how you experience your asexuality specifically. Feeling seen and understood is a big part of feeling loved, and for an ace person just coming to understand themselves, having someone to share that space of understanding with is everything. And the sharing on your part—the patience and time it takes to learn with your allo partner—will make them feel seen, too.

Then, reframe asexuality in the context of your relationship. It'll be easy to see asexuality as a new issue in your relationship, something that's come up that must be "dealt with" or "handled." Your partner may also come into the space of your new identity feeling as though there was a dishonesty in the past, or that your asexuality is changing the foundation. It's important to acknowledge these feelings, because they can be expected, but they can't be held as fact. Work together to reframe how asexuality is viewed in your relationship. It's not an issue to solve. It doesn't make the time before it a lie. Your relationship will struggle to succeed unless you and your partner—yes, *both* of you—consider your asexuality an important part of what makes you a good fit.

Finally, a harder thing: Mourn what's lost. It's okay for you both to feel as though you've lost something. In a way, you have. There's an understanding of your team that no longer holds true, an understanding that likely held a lot of hopes and expectations as well as a lot of struggles and fights and wounds. A really loving thing you can do for each other is to mourn the loss of that understanding, mourn the loss of those people you thought you were together. Support each other in that mourning process. Acknowledge what was great. Acknowledge what wasn't. And honor it for what it was: one chapter in the story of your life together.

Then, allow that chapter to be closed. Focus on the new one you can build together. I don't think there's a single thing you can do that would mean more or feel more loving than that. It's a powerful way to embrace and honor each other, and it's a gift you'll give each other in your relationship.

PART III

Asexuality and the World

Chapter 9
ASEXUALITY AND THE QUEER COMMUNITY

I attended my first Pride event at 45 years old.

I've been out as a queer person since I was 18, but until 45, I'd never attended Pride. It wasn't because I thought Pride was a bad thing, or because I was afraid of being seen at one or being thought of as queer. I've just had, thanks to a lifelong case of social anxiety disorder, a distaste for crowds and any extended social interaction that exceeded maybe ten minutes.

A few months after launching "Ace Dad Advice," the online ace education project that turned me into a Very Public Asexual, I received a Facebook invite from a friend of mine who was an organizer of our local Pride event.

"Hey Cody! Don't forget Pride is this weekend. You should come. I'd love to see you out there!"

"Do you wanna go to Pride?" I asked my husband.

He shot me a bit of side eye. This was clearly a trap. "*You* want to go to Pride?"

"Yeah," I said. "It's not like we're going to New York Pride. It's local. It's outside. And I've never been, and I don't know... It feels like this is the right time to go. Like I *should* go to Pride."

Within an hour, I had my ace astronaut T-shirt on and we were headed to Pride.

We found a spot not far from the main performance stage, close enough to get a good view of the performances and speakers but far enough from the crowds that it wouldn't raise my blood pressure.

There were so many *rainbows*. Rainbow flags, rainbow shirts, rainbow wigs, rainbow shoes. And every rainbow seemed to carry some queer person with it: gay folks, lesbian folks, bisexual folks, nonbinary folks, trans folks, a small group of folks flying the intersex flag, a couple of kids running and trailing the aromantic flag behind them. There was music and laughter and an abiding sense of joy.

"You doing okay?" my husband asked.

At that moment, a quartet of young people squeezed through a spot in the crowd and tumbled into the more open area we were standing in. They were all no more than 18 or 19 years old, clearly very close friends, all of them laughing wildly. Each wore an asexual flag tied around their necks, flapping behind them like capes. They had ace pins, ace T-shirts. One even had an ace hat.

I couldn't take my eyes off of them. They were so young, but they *knew* themselves. They knew who they were. And they not only knew themselves, but they felt enough pride in that knowledge to be *here*, in public, sharing that with everyone, sharing it with the world, wearing their asexuality like the cape of a superhero.

I thought they were incredible. In my eyes, they *were* superheroes.

One of them caught my eye and saw I was watching them. He looked down at my shirt for a second and smiled a tiny smile. "Nice shirt," he said, and went back to the safety and camaraderie of his friends. The one with the hat started to lead them away, and they vanished again into the sea of rainbows.

Belonging was something I've always struggled with feeling. I've always felt like an outsider, not quite fitting in anywhere: not in my family, not with my friends, not in the gay community, not with work colleagues. I've lived my life always feeling slightly off to the side and never really feeling like I've found my place. But that day at Pride, I felt belonging. I knew who I was. I knew who my people were. I knew where I fit in.

It was a little like meeting myself for the first time.

"Hey," my husband nudged again. "You okay?"

"Yeah," I said. "Definitely okay."

This chapter is all about asexuality and its place in the LGBTQIA+ community. We'll discuss why I prefer the word "queer" to describe that community. We'll explore why asexuals belong in that community. We'll consider whether or not you have to define yourself as queer when you're ace. And we'll explore a simple framework for taking your first steps into advocating for your queer community.

Let's talk about the word "queer"

Throughout this chapter (and in other sections of the book you've read so far), I use the word "queer" a lot. I use it to describe individuals. I use it to describe a larger community that holds space for those individuals. And I use it to describe certain ideas or constructs.

"Queer" is a word with a complicated history. It began as a simple word to describe something unusual or strange. In the nineteenth century, "queer" began to be used as a derogatory word, an insult cast at those who participated in same-sex sexual activity. "Queer" as an insult was primarily used against men who participated in same-sex sex and men who were perceived as acting in an overly feminine way. In the last few decades of the twentieth century, activists within the LGBTQIA+ community began to reclaim the word "queer," taking it back as a word of self- and community identification, turning it from an insult into an empowering descriptor.

Broadly today, "queer" is used as an encompassing term to describe individuals who live outside of cisgender (a person whose gender identity matches the sex they were assigned at birth), heterosexual experiences. "Queer" includes all of the communities that make up the LGBTQIA+ acronym: gay men, lesbians, bisexuals, transgender folks, nonbinary folks, asexuals, intersex folks, agender folks, aromantic folks, two-spirit folks, questioning folks, and more. If you are living outside of a cisgender heterosexual experience, "queer" is a word that holds space for you.

Not everyone within LGBTQIA+ circles feels comfortable with the reclaimed "queer." Some older members of the community who experienced years of abuse on the other end of that word may object to its use as a self- or community descriptor. Inasmuch as some members of the community find power and strength in the use of the word "queer," many community members find the word demeaning and painful. It's important to hold both truths when we think about and use the word "queer."

"Queer" also holds an important place when we talk about queer theory, the field of study that looks at how cultural norms around gender and sexuality privilege or oppress individuals, depending on whether they adhere to or subvert those norms. Queer theory uses that exploration as a foundation to imagine potential worlds where those cultural norms and all the tools that create binaries—groupings, labels, definitions, and the like—are removed in order to erase that oppression from the world. Queer theory is concerned with possibility and potentiality for all people, regardless of their gender or sexual expression. Much of this book would probably annoy queer theorists, but if you're interested in more radical imaginings for how queer folks can exist in the world, dive into queer theory.

I use "queer" to describe myself. I am a homoromantic asexual who uses he/they pronouns. While that language specifically describes my experience of sexuality and gender, it can be cumbersome language in everyday use. "Queer" provides me with a useful shorthand to speak to the different ways I inhabit queerness. I also use "queer" because it speaks to my membership in the broader community of people who inhabit minority gender and sexuality experiences. "Queer," while not having to work for everyone, can be a powerful bit of language to help you speak about your place in the world.

Who exactly is in the queer community?

The queer community holds space for a lot of folks.

So far in this chapter, you've seen me use the acronym LGBTQIA+ in reference to the community. That acronym is one of several variations you might see in reference to the community: LGBT, LGBTQ, LGBTQ+, LGBTQQIA, LGBTQQIP2SAA. All of these acronyms reach to describe, with varying degrees of specificity and completeness, the community of people that live queer lives, lives outside a cisgender, heterosexual experience.

That's the tie that binds the community together: living outside the cisgender, heterosexual experience. The queer community is for everyone the acronym highlights and everyone queer we haven't imagined yet.

The queer community includes communities of people who live sexual and romantic identity experiences outside of heterosexuality: gay, lesbian, bisexual, pansexual, asexual, aromantic, and more. The queer community also includes communities of people who live gender identity experiences outside of being cisgender: transgender, two-spirit, agender, nonbinary, genderqueer, androgynous, and more. The queer community also includes intersex folks (people who are born with physical sex characteristics that do not fit our binary ideas about gender), questioning folks (anyone still figuring out the way to articulate their experience of queerness), folks who reject labels and the binary constructions they create, and folks who simply consider themselves "queer."

That's a lot of people and experiences! If there is anything this section communicates, I hope it's that there is a vast array of experiences outside of being cisgender and heterosexual. There's so much diversity and so much variation, it's almost impossible to understand why our culture would believe that anything other than being cisgender or heterosexual is being broken. The queer community is the embodiment of our limitless range of possibilities, and the beauty those possibilities contain.

But why are asexuals part of the queer community?

Asexuality is included in the queer community because it is an experience of sexuality outside of heterosexuality.

Not experiencing or rarely experiencing sexual attraction, regardless of how one experiences romantic attraction and how one enters into relationships with other people, is a minority sexual experience. It sits outside of the expected heterosexual experience. That makes it a queer experience.

But what about asexuals who don't have sex? How are they queer?

Sexual activity does not define or legitimize someone's sexual orientation. You are who you are, even when you're not having sex. Gay people are still gay when they're not having sex. Straight people are still straight when they're not having sex. And asexual people continue to be asexual even if sex isn't a part of their lives. We can experience the inequities and injustices of being a sexual minority even if we aren't having sex. So those experiences are still queer. Sex-averse, sex-repulsed, sex-neutral, and sex-favorable ace folks have a rightful place in the queer community.

But asexuals don't really experience oppression or discrimination the way other queer people do. How are they queer?

First, the experience of oppression or discrimination does not define or legitimize someone's queer identity. Queer people are queer because they're living outside of cisgender, heterosexual norms. While oppression and discrimination are part of that outsider experience, they are not what defines that experience. Different parts of the queer community will experience oppression and discrimination in different ways and at varying degrees. And a queer person's other identities—for example, their race or whether or not they're disabled—will further complicate how they experience oppression and discrimination. Comparing oppression or using oppression as a way to decide who belongs and who doesn't is never fruitful. It's of course important to acknowledge and center people when their part of our community is more at risk than others, and we should be aware of when our identities or intersections make navigating oppression and discrimination easier. But every queer person is othered by their queerness. The nature and experience of that may change from community to community, but there are always consequences for living outside cisgender, heterosexual norms.

Asexual people experience many forms of discrimination. We can be socially ostracized and infantilized by our allosexual peers. We can be inundated with messages from the people around us who say we are broken or stunted. We can be medicalized or pressured into therapy unnecessarily. Asexuals can be pressured by their partners into sex they don't really want to have, be subjected to unwanted sexual advances, harassment, and, in the most extreme cases, corrective rape. Ace and aro-ace folks that forgo traditional romantic relationships can face the social stigmas that single people face in our culture. While these injustices and hardships may not mirror the oppression other communities face, they are real and tangible harms for ace people. The queer community can hold space for all queer people and the unique oppressions and discriminations they face.

But asexuals can pass as heterosexuals, so they're not really queer

"Passing" as heterosexual is not *being* heterosexual. So, no matter the outward appearance of someone or of their relationship, they are always as queer as who they are on the inside.

Asexual people who are heteroromantic—who date and form relationships that socially code as heterosexual—are still asexual. The disposition of their relationship and how it is perceived by people outside of it does not change their asexuality. In the same vein, asexual or aro-ace people who do not pursue relationships—who are then assumed to be heterosexual because of cultural norms—are not less asexual because of that assumption.

How we are *perceived* by the world does not change the truth or legitimacy of who we *are*.

There is something to say here, however, about perception and "passing," the ability or tendency of a person to be seen as a member of an identity group they don't inhabit, which allows them to bypass some of their actual identity group's oppressions and discriminations. We should be aware of the ways in which we "pass," particularly when it allows us to avoid some harm that others in our community cannot.

For example, I'm an asexual man who has relationships with men. That is my reality all of the time, and I can experience the harm that sometimes comes with those identities. But I'm also a six-foot-two cisgender white man with a thick beard and a lot of tattoos. In most situations, I can pass as straight. I don't actively seek out that perception, but it's a reality I acknowledge, and that perception, that passing, can, in some situations, lessen the harm I experience as an asexual man who has relationships with men. That passing doesn't change the truth of my queerness, but it does mean I experience that particular queerness in a different way than someone who cannot pass.

Being aware of the ways in which we can inhabit less dangerous spaces of queer experience while others are existing in more dangerous ones is important. It helps recognize who in our community is most in need, and it reminds us, even when we're all in the same big queer boat, that who we are outside of our queerness exerts powerful influence on how we move through the world.

But doesn't "queer" mean "gay?"

"Queer" is not synonymous with "gay." You don't have to be gay to be queer.

In the history of the word "queer," its usage as an insult or slur was mainly aimed at homosexual men or men who presented more femininely than was socially acceptable. As a slur, it developed a strong association with gayness. So even though the word has evolved in its usage, for many people it still holds on to those older associations.

"Queer" also retains those associations with gayness due to the disparities in visibility of queer people in our culture. The most visible people in the queer community—the most seen in media, the most represented in positions of power and advocacy, the most impacted positively by the legislative gains we've made in the area of queer rights—are gay men and women. So, when "queer" is used to describe our community, most people think of gay men and women first.

Remember: The queer community holds space for everyone experiencing the world outside of the cisgender, heterosexual experience. So "queer" is so much more than just "gay." Queer is heterosexual transgender folks. Queer is heteroromantic asexual folks. Queer is panromantic nonbinary folks. Queer is aro-ace folks. Queer is not limited to a variation on a gay experience. Queer is a richer, more vibrant spectrum of experience.

Do I have to call myself queer?

No, you don't have to use the word "queer" to define yourself.

Remember when we talked about labels being tools, not tests? Labels exist to help you describe your experience and to build community with other folks who share your experience. They are never an imperative. You are never required to use a label. You are never pressured to rearrange yourself to fit one.

There are still plenty of people who feel uncomfortable with "queer" as a bit of identity language due to their negative experiences with the word as a slur. Reclaimed or not, for some people, the ugly history of "queer" is too much to overcome.

And some just feel as though the word doesn't fit them. I've met heteroromantic asexual folks who feel that "queer" isn't theirs to use. I know many people in the queer community who only feel comfortable exclusively using more specific identity labels. "Queer" is too broad or unclear for them.

No one has to call themselves "queer." But I do think it's important to always allow space for the word to be used. It's cool to not be comfortable with it yourself, but don't try to limit others who use it. For many of us, "queer" is a powerful and useful bit of identity language. It's a word that empowers us, describes us, and helps us find our people.

Queer means action!

My first very openly queer friend in college was a ferociously smart and outspoken lesbian named Chilli. I adored Chilli, even though she only put up with me because we ran in the same theater circles. I'm pretty sure she thought I was hopelessly banal, only cool because I could quote Sondheim better than the other theater geeks.

Chilli identified as queer, which was unusual for our group. She was also deeply involved in local queer politics, which, in our small Southern college town, weren't exactly electrifying. But she was always keeping us informed on anti-queer ballot initiatives at the city level and making sure we knew which pro-queer candidates to vote for. She volunteered at the local gay health clinic and worked closely with local HIV educators. Her queerness was more engaged than any of us, and I very much admired her for it.

Over beers one night at a closing-night cast party, I asked her why she used "queer."

"Isn't it an insult?" I asked. "I got called 'queer' all the time as a kid. I don't think I want to call *myself* one. Why not just 'lesbian'?"

"Sure, I'm a lesbian," she said. "*Technically* that's right. But I don't know. 'Lesbian' doesn't feel like it says everything I want a word to say about me. 'Queer' feels more right. 'Queer' is like 'lesbian plus action,' you know? 'Queer' feels like identity with a little bit of troublemaking."

As someone who now uses "queer" more than any other word to describe myself, I'm on Chilli's side on this. I use "queer" because it encompasses all of the ways in which I'm a gender and sexual minority, and it connects me and my specific queernesses to the larger community of queer people I belong to. Plus, as Chilli explained to me, there is something actionable about the word "queer," some implied spirit of political and social engagement. "Queer" can feel like "I am *and* I do."

In that spirit of active queerness, I wanted this book to include something about advocacy and the urge some of us may have to inhabit our queerness in a highly public way. While it's not required of anyone in our community, there's something admirable about stepping up and speaking out for your people. Whether it's on the front lines of a protest with signs and shouts or it's correcting aphobic microaggressions on Twitter, you might want to take your queerness one step further into the world and work to improve that world for future queer folks.

Here are a few things to remember:

Anger is okay. Anger has a purpose. Don't let anyone tell you that you shouldn't feel anger about the way asexual and other queer people are treated in the world. When confronted with the injustice, hatred, discrimination, and violence our community faces, what other emotion could there be? Anger is an appropriate response to injustice, and while we should never let our anger consume us or allow us to harm the people around us, anger can be a powerful fuel for our advocacy. When injustice starts a fire in you, use that fire to light the way to something better.

Advocacy doesn't have to be big to matter. You don't have to write a book or stage a protest or make popular art or have huge social media accounts to engage in advocacy that matters. Small things count, too. In fact, small things can sometimes count more than the big things. The power you have as an individual ace person to enact change is enormous. Simply being in the world and being ace to the people around you—at whatever level you're comfortable with—can change someone's mind about asexuality. And if you change the mind of one person, you've already achieved something monumental. Change is change, no matter the scale.

Advocacy and activism are acts of love. Activists and advocates often get accused of being troublemakers, disruptors, and disrespectful agitators who just want attention or who just want to get other people upset. And sure, disruption is often the name of the game, but activists and advocates create those disruptions and make that trouble out of love. Advocacy and activism happen because we *love:* We love the people experiencing injustice, we love the communities that are expressing need, we love the ideas of fairness and justice for everyone, we love the vision of an equitable world that treats everyone as they deserve to be treated. The kind of love that fuels advocacy and activism is, to me, the most radical kind of love. It's a love that's willing to fight, to get bruised and bloodied, to extend yourself past the boundaries of your own life, to offer up a part of yourself in order to help and improve the lives of others. That's some serious love, and even if it's not the thing we choose to do ourselves, we should always lift up the people who do.

Chapter 10

ACE IN THE WORLD

I downloaded TikTok because of my barber, Todd.

"You should do it. It's a lot of fun," he said.

"Ehh, I don't know," I said. Telling him he was out of his mind while he was in the middle of making sure my hair looked presentable to the world for the next few weeks didn't seem like a smart move. "I'm old, you know. TikTok is for the kids. What am I gonna do on TikTok?"

"It's not just the kids," he said. "It's everyone. And everyone's just sharing the things they're passionate about, the things that excite them. I've met some really cool people on there. *I'm* on there, so..."

I love Todd. He's easily one of the coolest humans I know. He's led a very eclectic life that's bounced him around an assortment of creative professions like music, coffee, and painting. He's covered in tattoos, beautiful work that's not only visually stunning but also speaks to who he is as a person. He likes to portray himself as a pretty dark soul—I mean, he does have a very wicked sense of humor—but he's also one of the kindest, most open people I've ever met. *And* he's out-of-this-world talented as a barber, so it's really a win for everyone.

"Okay, yeah, but you're *actually* cool," I tell him. "I am in my mid-forties. I read a lot of books. I watch a lot of horror movies. The most interesting thing about me is that I'm queer, and that, these days, is not even all that interesting."

"I think you'd be surprised," he said. "TikTok. Do it."

Partially because I was curious and partially because I really just want Todd to like me, I downloaded TikTok and started making videos.

At first, they were really dumb, just me documenting uninteresting things I was doing during the day. Occasionally I'd try one of the trends or use one of the trending sounds. I'd try dueting or stitching videos, just to better understand how the app worked.

One day at work, I stitched a video of this girl asking a question: "What's something that feels both gay and homophobic?"

My reply: "The reaction I get from guys when I tell them I'm ace."

I sent that little video out into the world, and I went back to work, assuming nobody would see it, nobody would care about it, and I'd return to TikTok later to make another video that would be consumed by the void.

A few hours later, I returned to a huge jump in my follower count, a massive amount of interaction on that video and tens of thousands of views. There were hundreds of comments, many of them echoing the same sentiment:

- *I'm sorry I'm so emotional, you're the first elder ace I've ever seen.*
- *This is the first time I've ever seen an older ace. I'm legitimately crying.*
- *Seeing another male ace who is not 16 is doing a lot for my mental state right now.*
- *You are one of the first elder ace members I've seen on this app. You have no idea what that means to me.*

It was a pretty emotional moment for me, too. Up to that point, my asexuality had been something private. It wasn't a *secret*—I was out to my husband, my friends, and other people close to me—but it wasn't something that interacted with the world. It wasn't *public*. So I never had to think about the ways my asexuality would rub up against all of the people and ideas that moved outside of my personal circles. I never had to grapple with what it meant to be ace in the world.

But now, because of a TikTok, my asexuality—and how someone like me, with my other identities and other realities, inhabits that asexuality—was firmly in the world. Being seen. Being considered. Being contextualized. Being judged. Those interactions, the ones that go smoothly and the ones that produce sometimes unbearable friction, open a door to consider more than just how asexuality affects me and the people I have relationships with. Being ace *in the world* reveals things *about the world*, and what's revealed helps us to better define our place in it.

This chapter explores some of the things being ace in the world reveals about the world. We'll look at some of the cultural constructs that asexuality questions. We'll look at how asexuality can inform and is informed by its interactions with these norms. And we'll explore a way of thinking about how asexuality interacts with our other identities that will make us better members of our community.

The ideas and social constructs explored here aren't the only ones that are at work in the world. This is a very small sampling of the social and cultural structures that are operating around us. The ones included here are a couple of the biggies, and they're the ones that make the most sense to include in this exploration of asexuality. It's also important to remember that these concepts and constructs are much deeper and much more complicated than this short chapter can detail. This isn't meant to make you a scholar on the subject. It's only meant to give you a basic primer and nudge you in the direction of learning more.

Compulsory sexuality

Compulsory sexuality is the pervasive social and cultural idea that everyone has or wants frequent sex. While all kinds of sex can be expected under compulsory sexuality, it prefers and favors sex of a more acceptable kind: heterosexual, monogamous sex. But across all kinds of sex, the expectation is the same. If you're a person, sex is an important part of your life.

This idea is everywhere. Think of how often sex and sexual imagery is used in commercials and advertising. Think of how often sex is depicted in movies and TV shows, even when the stories have nothing to do with sex at all. Think of all the magazine articles shouting about "50 ways to improve your sex life!" or "How to save your sexless relationship!" Think of all the talk show episodes, podcasts, books, YouTube channels, advice columns, workshops, classes, and therapists focused on solving the problems in your sex life so that you can have all the sex you want and need and *deserve*.

Compulsory sexuality also shows up in more structural ways. Sex is used to determine which relationships are more prized and privileged in our culture. Relationships that include sex are the ones that are encouraged. They're the relationships that are considered to "have a future." And they're the relationships we've built institutions around, namely marriage, to provide the people in them with economic and social advantages. A product of sex—children—is also prized in our culture, and we've developed institutional advantages for those people who decide to have kids. You can have kids without having sex, but if you choose to have them without sex, you face a lot of administrative and bureaucratic obstacles and considerable financial investment in order to have them. None of that is true if your road to parenthood is a little s-e-x.

Compulsory sexuality hitches our place in the world to sex. If we adhere to the demands of compulsory sexuality, either because we instinctively desire to or we decide to, our status in the culture is elevated. If we don't adhere to the demands—if we decide to not prioritize or participate in sex, if we inhabit a body that doesn't want and desire sex, or if we inhabit a body that cannot physically have sex—then we will be relegated to a lower cultural status. We will be seen as broken. We will be pitied. We will be rendered invisible.

Compulsory sexuality is what makes asexual people seek out hormone treatments or counseling. It's what makes asexual people feel responsible to provide sexual activity to a partner when they don't want to or to allow and forgive a partner for infidelities. Compulsory sexuality is what underpins the harassment and sexual violence asexual people sometimes face when they assert their desire not to have sex.

Asexuality rejects the ideas of compulsory sexuality. Asexuality demonstrates that human experience isn't irrevocably tied to sex. You can be a person without wanting sex. You can be a person without *having* sex. Your personhood is complete without either of those things. And sex is not something owed to anyone in your life, and it is not something someone has a right to demand or take from you. Asexuality demands that our value as individuals not be tied up in our relationship to sex. It asserts that we should not be devalued, relegated to lower social statuses, harmed, or rendered invisible because of it.

Allonormativity

Allonormativity is the pervasive social and cultural idea that all people are allosexual and experience sexual attraction. It may sound very similar to compulsory sexuality, but it speaks to a different set of cultural assumptions. While compulsory sexuality is concerned with whether or not people are engaging in sex, allonormativity is focused on whether or not you're feeling sexual attraction. Allonormativity asserts its demands on you whether or not you're having sex. It's considering your status regardless of your behavior.

Allonormativity shows up in our lives right from the start and follows us relentlessly into adulthood. Think of how we respond when babies or toddlers form connections and play together: "Oooh look, they've got crushes on each other!" Think of how we draw a line between childhood and adulthood with the experience of sexual attraction, and how we consider people who don't express or share their experience of sexual attraction the kind of people who just need to "grow up." Think of how often, when someone expresses any kind of interest in another person, it's assumed they find that person sexually attractive. Think of how we decide whether or not someone is "relationship worthy" based on whether or not there's mutual sexual attraction.

Allonormativity assumes a universal human experience when it comes to sexual attraction: We all have it and we all experience it. It assumes that experience of sexual attraction completes us as people, actualizes us, matures us. That completeness is privileged whether or not sexual behavior is present.

Allonormativity underpins so much of the discrimination asexual people face. Its belief that sexual attraction is a human default innately places asexual people in a realm outside of basic humanness. We're either somehow less than human—which holds up the ideas we're immature, infantile, otherwise unformed people—or we're broken humans. Justifying the idea that asexual people are broken is one of allonormativity's most powerful talents. So many of us believe we are broken, move through the world as though we're broken, construct relationships through apologies for that brokenness.

Asexuality, however, is not a state of brokenness. Asexuality is a full, whole human experience. And lived that way, as a complete way of relating to sex and sexual attraction, asexuality offers a sharp rebuttal to the messages of allonormativity. Asexuality says you do not have to experience sexual attraction to be complete. You do not have to experience sexual attraction to build worthwhile relationships. You do not have to experience sexual attraction to be fully yourself.

Amatonormativity

Amatonormativity is the pervasive social and cultural idea that all human beings desire and seek out love and romance and aspire to express those emotions in the context of lifelong monogamous relationships. Amatonormativity not only contextualizes romance as a default human experience, one that defines our humanness, but it also creates a rigid relationship hierarchy that assigns negative moral judgment or diminished value to every relationship structure outside of monogamy.

Amatonormativity shows up in our lives in a number of ways. It underpins the generational pressure in families for younger people to pursue marriage. It's the reason why marriage is seen as an ideal, an expected goal, a necessity for a complete life. Amatonormativity is why we culturally view friendships as a lower rung of relationships, as relationships we "graduate" from when we enter into romantic relationships, as opposed to equal and complete relationships on the same level as romantic relationships. It's why single people are viewed as unfortunate, unhappy, or lonely. Amatonormativity is why marriages are afforded legal and economic privileges in our society (the legal status afforded married couples over other relationships, tax breaks for married couples, and the like).

For alloromantic asexual folks (asexual folks who experience romantic attraction), amatonormativity complicates the kind of relationships outside of monogamy that are pursuable. It pressures alloromantic asexual folks to conform to exclusivity and monogamy, even if those ideas don't form the basis for the kinds of relationships that might be desirable or workable. Amatonormativity exerts a stronger and more detrimental pressure on aro-ace folks, however. It applies a double insistence of brokenness on aro-ace folks: Not only are aro-ace folks unable to meet the sexual defaults of being a human, but they are also missing the mark on the romantic defaults, too. And amatonormativity erases the validity of non-romance focused relationships, like friendships or queerplatonic relationships, which leaves aro-ace folks with no respected or socially supported relationship options that don't require them to pretend at romance.

Asexuality, and in particular aromantic asexuality, rejects the assertions of amatonormativity. Exclusive, monogamous romantic relationships are not the only viable and successful kinds of relationships. Viable and successful relationships can leave out sex, open the door to consensual non-monogamy, reject exclusivity in exchange for multiple romantic partners, reconstruct the ways sex and love coexist in a relationship, or forgo love and sex entirely. Asexuality and aromanticism both tell us that love and sex aren't central to happiness. Love and sex aren't central to humanness. They're one option of many.

Heteronormativity

Heteronormativity is the pervasive social and cultural idea that heterosexual relationships, particularly monogamous heterosexual marriages, are the ideal relationships for people to inhabit. Other relationships—relationships that deviate from heterosexuality, relationships that are structured in non-exclusive ways, or relationships that question the gender binary—are less than ideal and ultimately harmful to society at large. Heteronormativity sets up a powerful cultural system of privilege and punishment, the goal of which is to keep people in line performing behaviors it feels most benefit society.

Heteronormativity is everywhere. Heterosexual couples are the only couples that can comfortably be open about their relationships in all social and professional situations. Our media and art almost universally focus on heterosexual couples when they explore relationships. Our laws are constructed to confer many benefits on heterosexual married couples, particularly those married couples who choose to have children. For most of history, same-sex marriages were forbidden by law, and the inclusion of same-sex couples in civil marriage continues to be a hugely contested cultural issue. Non-monogamous relationships are culturally shunned. Polyamorous families receive no legal protections. And queerness itself remains varyingly illegal at all levels of government all around the world.

For many asexual people, heteronormativity inflicts punishment on most aspects of the lives they inhabit. Whether it's the way they build relationships or simply the way they occupy their minds and bodies, heteronormativity doesn't approve of asexuality. And with its incredible cultural power, pressures ace folks to deny their asexuality. It can pressure ace folks into monogamous relationships when consensual non-monogamy would better suit the way they love. It can pressure aro-ace folks into romantic relationships when queerplatonic relationships or no relationship at all would better suit them. It can force ace people into hiding their aceness and wearing the drag of heterosexuality in order to move through the world without judgment or scorn.

Exclusive heterosexual marriages that reinforce the gender binary are not a default and are not an ideal. Asexuality provides one of the reminders across queer experience that heteronormativity does not speak the truth. Asexuality reminds us more options exist. Asexuality reminds us more possibilities can be imagined.

Chrononormativity

Chrononormativity is a way to describe the way culture uses time, in coordination with other normative forces like allonormativity or amatonormativity, to exert "life deadlines" on individuals in an attempt to ensure they provide the maximum benefit to the society at large. Chrononormativity suggests that we organize life milestones, and assign moral values to meeting or missing those milestones, at certain times so that we can serve social needs before our individual needs. It's a way to not only encourage individuals to adhere to cultural norms but to also encourage individuals to achieve the goals of those norms at specific points in our lives. If we do, we're helping the machinery of society run more smoothly, even if doing so isn't the best for us.

Chrononormativity shows up any time we're told or are made to feel like we're falling behind our peers in hitting life goals. "You should have done that by now!" or "It's time for you to get serious about...!" are examples of chrononormativity rearing its head. It shows up in the idea that certain behaviors are tied to certain times of our life. "You've outgrown that!" or "You're too young to understand that!" is chrononormativity. "Marry and have kids when you're young!" or "You're not really an adult until you buy a house!" or "You're a grownup and you need to stop fooling around with that hobby!" are all examples of chrononormativity. Any time culture suggests that an experience or an individual reality can only be valid or real when it's tied to a specific time in life, that's chrononormativity.

For asexual folks, chrononormativity compounds the pressures exerted on us by other cultural norms. Not only are we pushed to adhere to the demands of things like allonormativity or compulsory sexuality, we're also judged by the speed at which we achieve that conformity. You're a sex-repulsed asexual choosing to not have sex? Not only are you falling short of the norms of allonormativity, but if you remain sexless as you move into your adult years—years in which sexual activity is assumed by chrononormativity—you're falling behind. You're not "growing up." You're a sex-neutral asexual who chooses consensual non-monogamy over a monogamous marriage for your relationships? Not only are you falling short of our culture's amatonormative ideas, but if you continue to eschew monogamy, you're behaving as a reckless, selfish child instead of a mature adult. Chrononormativity, in cooperation with the other norms, is at the core of why asexual people are often infantilized or seen as defenseless, childish, or incapable of adult responsibilities.

Living truthfully and authentically as an ace person pushes back against chrononormativity. Our asexual lives show that you don't have to achieve certain sexual or relationship milestones at specific points in order to have a full, adult life. We can reject the norms completely. We can focus parts of our lives on things other than relationships and sex. We can be fully functioning, mature members of society without following the timeline society expects of us. We can build our own timelines, and in doing so, build our own lives.

Intersectionality

So far in this chapter, we've looked at these large social constructs through a lens of impacting asexual people as a community. And for the most part, you can view these constructs that way. As we've explored them, asexuality interacts with these constructs in specific ways that can be observed across many people within our community. But that observation is generalized: it's assuming a *general* asexual person.

But that's not the way the world works. That's not how people exist in the world. Our community is made up of many different kinds of people, with wildly different backgrounds and experiences, with many other identities they inhabit outside of their asexuality. And if we are to be truly thoughtful about the asexual experience, we have to think about those other identities and experiences and how they impact the experience of asexuality.

Intersectionality is a framework for thinking about these things. Coined and articulated by Kimberlé Crenshaw, a law professor and social theorist, in 1989, intersectionality is a way of looking at an individual's intersecting identities and how those intersections impact that individual's experience of oppression. We can be disadvantaged across multiple identities, intersectionality argues, so understanding how those intersections compound oppression or alleviate oppression is important to truly understanding a person's experience of the world.

An asexual individual isn't only asexual. An asexual person also inhabits other identities: their race, their gender, their class, their religion, whether they are disabled or not, whether they are neurodivergent or not. That asexual person's experience of asexuality—and specifically their experience of the oppression and discrimination asexuals face—will change based on how their other identities intersect with their asexuality. Black asexual women will face different forms of oppression than white asexual men do. Disabled asexual folks will experience different forms of oppression than their non-disabled asexual counterparts. Who we are outside of asexuality colors how we experience asexuality. And our experience as asexual people will bear weight on and color our experience of our other identities.

We won't ever fully liberate ourselves from the damage of the social constructs explored here unless we think of them intersectionally. We won't fully understand how allonormativity impacts asexual people unless we're considering how Black asexual people experience it differently from white asexual people, how asexual women experience it differently from asexual men, and the like. We can't combat amatonormativity unless we're designing solutions that address how transgender asexual folks experience it as opposed to cisgender ace folks, how neurodivergent ace folks experience it as opposed to neurotypical ace folks.

And we have to think about how multiple identities build oppression. Black asexual women have specific experiences of oppression that are different from Black asexual men. Neurodivergent nonbinary ace folks have specific experiences of oppression that are different from neurotypical cisgender ace folks. Every identity we occupy is a new lens that magnifies or de-magnifies the oppression we experience, and as we project our experience through the multiplicity of lenses we inhabit, the view of how we are shaped by the world is changed. Intersectionality is a way for us to think about that process, and it's essential if we are to achieve an equitable world for all ace people.

So...what do we do with all of this?

When I was writing this chapter, I was on a vacation with all the members of our constellation, my chosen family: my husband, Neil; his partner, Dan; and my partner, Scott. Dan and Scott are long-distance partners to us, so this was the first trip the four of us were able to make together, and it was a smashing success.

Dan and Scott were preparing a dinner for the constellation on our last night together, and we were talking about the unconventional nature of our chosen family. We're an uncommon bunch. I'm asexual. The rest of the constellation identifies as gay. Neil is exploring some nonbinary dimensions to his gender identity. And while we're all practicing polyamory, we're not all in romantic relationships. My relationship with Dan and Neil's relationship with Scott are more queerplatonic in nature, and Scott and Dan are just beginning their friendship. But we're hoping to build a four-person family that doesn't look like anything you'd see in a Hallmark holiday movie.

"We buck a lot of the norms you're writing about," Scott said.

"That we do," I replied.

"We probably buck *all* of them in one way or another," Dan said.

"I've always found it interesting that that's usually the case," Scott said. "You're not just finding people breaking one of the normative ways of thinking. You break one, you end up breaking more, breaking them all."

"You take the first leap," Neil said, "and every leap after is easier."

"You just have to learn that the norms are lies," Dan said.

"I think two things are important," I said. "And you need both of them to take the leap. You can't take the leap without both. You have to know the norms are *lies*, and you have to know the norms are *harmful*. You can know they're lies, but if you don't think they're dangerous, if you don't think they hurt people, they hurt *you*, you can maybe just go along with them because it's easier. When you know they're also dangerous, you know you can't stay put. You have to leap. To save yourself. To save your people."

"You're putting that in the book, right?" Neil said.

"It's got to go in the book," Dan said.

Scott walked around the kitchen counter and kissed me on the forehead. "Put it in the book."

My constellation—my three beautiful guys with beautiful hearts and an abundance of optimism and bravery—is an example of what we do with this.

We learn to recognize the cultural norms that are working on us and around us, shaping the way we think about ourselves, shaping the way we think about the world, nudging our decisions in the direction of conformity.

We recognize that those norms are causing us harm and that the harm isn't within us. The harm isn't something broken in us. It's the world and its demands.

Then we take that knowledge and leap.

We leap into a version of ourselves that embraces and loves and *celebrates* our queerness.

We leap into relationships that are structured to fulfill us, to allow us the space to love the way we love.

We leap into communities of people that exist the way we do, that have sex the way we do, that love the way we do, that build families the way we do, and we leap into those communities with joy, not shame.

Chapter 11

FINDING YOUR ACE JOY

Remember my first coming out when I was 18? The letter, the Sunday dinner, the really awkward conversation?

About two weeks later, summer arrived, and I started a part-time job at the auto repair shop my dad managed. I didn't do any actual mechanic-type stuff—I was bad at that stuff then, and I am bad at it now—but I did handle some of the administrative tasks the shop required. It was very basic stuff: I created work orders. I filed parts invoices. I called customers to let them know their repairs were done.

One afternoon, my dad and I were the only two people in the shop, and I was finishing up a few invoices from the day. He came into the office and sat down across the desk from me.

"Can I ask you a question about...what we talked about the other day?"

I wasn't prepared for this. We hadn't said a thing about my coming out since it happened. I half expected we'd just pretend it hadn't happened at all. So it coming up, unexpectedly in this very weird context, took me by surprise.

"Yeah, uh. Sure." I took a little breath and held it, bracing for whatever was coming.

"I just want to know, does...the thing we talked about...does it make you happy?"

I didn't know what to say. I'd never thought about it. I knew all of the other feelings that being gay made me feel: anxious, scared, self-conscious, unsure. I knew that being gay felt hard and terrifying. I knew that it had, up to that point, kind of felt like a battle.

But did it make me *happy*?

I remembered what my friend James had said about not wanting to live an illusion. I thought about how, even though the repercussions made me fearful, I felt so much relief, so much comfort in telling the truth about myself. And not just telling the truth to other people, but telling the truth *about* myself *to* myself. Being honest about what I was feeling felt wonderful. It felt freeing. It felt full of possibility.

"Yeah." My voice was really small, and I couldn't look my dad in the eye while I said it. "It does make me happy. I feel... It makes me feel like me."

It was quiet for a moment. I shifted my gaze up to meet his glance.

"Then that's all that matters to us. That you're happy. We don't understand it, but we'll figure it out."

That conversation with my dad was one of the most important lessons of my life. I've lived everything through the lens of that conversation and that idea: that finding our happiness is the most important thing. Everything else—the obstacles, the setbacks, the things we don't understand, the things that come out of nowhere, our shortcomings, our mistakes, what people say or think or do to us—is something we will just figure out.

I wanted to end this book with a chapter dedicated to the joy in being asexual. The joy in letting go of the doubts and fears we held in the past. The joy in authentically living our truth in the present. The joy in envisioning a future for ourselves.

All of those things are possible for us. All of those things are a part of being ace.

The past really hurt. How am I supposed to let that go?

Many of us in the queer community feel we've lived two lives.

There's a life we live not knowing who we are, feeling broken and wrong, feeling like a stranger in our own skin. We're out of step with the world around us. We have no language for our own experience. We endure the rejection, the hate, and the violence of the world. It's a life we live wounded, a life we live damaged.

Then there's a life we live aware of who we are, feeling known to ourselves, feeling validated and complete, feeling embraced by the community of others who exist in the world as we do. We have words for how we're different. We find pride instead of shame in that difference. We're in step with ourselves, no matter what the world thinks. It's a life we live whole.

No matter how far we get in that second life, we're always carrying around the first one. We scoop up the pieces of that wounded person in our hands, pieces that are razor sharp to the touch, and say, "But, look! Yeah, I'm doing great now. But this was what I was! Look at this damaged person. Look at who I was!" We carry that around, and we cut ourselves on the pieces.

It hurts to carry that wounded version of us. But we can't stop carrying it. No matter how far we get, no matter who we become, that first life remains a part of us. Without it, we'd never have a chance to experience that second life. But collecting the cuts from carrying that first life ensures that a little part of us, no matter how comfortable we get in our own skin, is always a little bit wounded.

We have to find a way to carry that first life that doesn't leave scars on the second.

Have you ever heard of kintsugi?

Kintsugi, which means "golden repair," is a centuries-old Japanese art of repairing broken pottery vessels with gold. According to art historians, this practice began when a fifteenth-century Japanese shogun sent a broken tea bowl back to China for repairs. It was returned in a state that made the shogun very unhappy. The cracks were mended with unattractive metal staples.

So local artisans came up with a solution that was more pleasing to the eye. They created a specially blended lacquer that was stained with gold dust to rejoin the broken pieces. Now, instead of being covered in ugly metal staples, a repaired vessel was adorned with streaks of gold that twisted like branches across the face of the vessel. Yes, it was once a broken vessel, but it ended up being more beautiful (and more valuable) than it was before it was broken.

That's how we have to treat the first life we lead. We have to take the sharp pieces of the hard parts of our life and knit them together again, patch the cracks over with a bit of gold lacquer, and try to look at that wounded life through the eyes of repair.

Yes, it's painful to not know you're ace. Feeling different from everyone else sucks. The years you spend questioning, wondering, and feeling confused are really hard. It hurts to have people reject you, diminish you, tell you you're crazy or sick, immature or broken. I understand how you can look at that and think, *I don't want to make that beautiful. There's nothing beautiful about any of that.*

But that first life, for all its darkness, is also a life with some beautiful things in it.

Think about the persistence it takes to question and research and ask questions and think really deeply about what you feel and experience.

Think about the strength it takes to push through the fear, to soldier through the confusion, to wrestle with the doubts.

Think about the resilience it takes to own your difference when every message in the world is telling you that your difference makes you wrong or bad or broken.

Think about the courage it takes to admit the truth to yourself, to speak that truth to another person, to become someone and something new.

Those things are beautiful. Those things are *you*.

Those things, if you acknowledge them and honor them, are the gold lacquer that can repair the sharp pieces of that first life. So you can carry it around without getting cut. So you can live that second life as joyfully as you want.

You are more than your struggle

I'll be the first to admit that some of this really sucks. And, hopefully without adding insult to injury, some of it can really suck for a long, long time.

I still have days when I struggle hard. I have days when my insecurities about my worth and value to my partners is overwhelming. The internalized negativity I swallowed for decades can come bubbling up at the drop of a hat, making me depressed, anxious, and unbearably hard on myself. I can spend all day making affirming videos about loving your asexuality and sending encouraging messages to young people reassuring them that their asexuality is awesome, and I can still, in the quiet of my home office, wonder if I'm broken after all.

Anyone who dares to embrace a life outside of the cisgender, heterosexual norms that operate around us is going to face an uphill battle. The world has a lot invested in you simply playing by "the rules." It's not going to make it easy for you to step outside the box. So we have to make room for the struggle, because the struggle is going to be there whether we like it or not. We have to accept it as another passenger on the ride we're taking.

"You're telling me I have to just get used to things being miserable?" No. Not exactly. We don't have to get *used* to it. We just have to know that's sometimes how things will be. We have to keep working and growing and evolving past the stuff that sucks—a lengthy and often slow process, but each of us can get there!—while not getting stuck in the stuff that sucks.

So remember: You are more than your struggle.

When the days are hard, those days don't define you. When you struggle with insecurity or shame, those feelings don't define you. When you're anxious or depressed, those experiences don't define you. They can feel like the whole world. They can feel like forever. But they're only right now. They're only right here. They will pass.

So be kind to yourself when you're having a hard time with your asexuality. You haven't failed. You haven't let the asexual community down. You're still all the other cool things you are and do and feel in the world. You'll reach the other side of your struggle in time. It's not everything you are.

Asexuality is something you *live*

This one's brief, but I think it's important.

Asexuality isn't just a collection of terms and labels and definitions. It's not just academic. It's not just theory.

Asexuality is something we *live*.

Everything we've discussed in this book is important, but the most important thing is the life you go out and lead. The person you are, the friendships you nurture, the romances you develop, the work you do, the communities you build, the families you cultivate, the art you make, the other lives you touch—these are the most important things.

And when you do them as an ace person, out or not, you're defining what it means to be ace. You're the best representation we could ever have! You being you in the world does more for asexual people as a whole than any book or YouTube video or social media account or Twitter thread could ever achieve.

The life you live helps shape our community's story.

So...get out there and live a cool life! Live a life that brings you joy. Live a life that excites you. Live a life that leaves a mark, however small, on the world.

If you do that, you're helping our community leave a mark on the world too.

You have a future

Not long after I graduated high school, I was still in the closet, and I was working a job entirely wrong for me—retail associate in the china and bridal departments at a local department store—and I was eager to take a first step into some kind of queer existence.

The only problem was I didn't know any queer people. And if

I did know any queer people, I didn't realize they were queer. So I didn't know where exactly to turn. There was only one place I knew of that was remotely queer, the only bar I knew as a gay bar—a bar called C'est la Guerre!

C'est la Guerre! was infamous in my small Southern town. It was situated in a part of town that people considered "the bad part," which was just a polite way to say "poor and predominantly Black and queer." There was nothing inherently bad about this part of town. It just didn't look like the suburbs, which, in the South, then and now, is cause for suspicion and scorn. C'est la Guerre! was situated at the center of the action, at an intersection of two main town roads, casually called Four Corners.

It was the kind of bar my parents would drive by and say "Look, Cody, look. That's where the homos go!" and laugh.

(I'm not kidding. That's actually how I learned C'est la Guerre! was a gay bar.)

Well, if C'est la Guerre! was where the homos went, then it was apparently the place for me. And you have to start somewhere, right?

So, one night after work, I got in my car, and instead of heading home, I drove downtown to Four Corners. I parked outside the bar, took a few deep breaths, and went inside.

C'est la Guerre! (which means "That's war!" in French) lived up to its name. It was the shoddiest, darkest, dirtiest establishment I'd ever been in. The place had barely any bar furniture. There were a few thin bar tables with rickety, mismatched barstools lined up along the wall. There were two square tables with maybe three chairs between them over near the hall that led to the bathrooms. And the walls were decorated with fading, out-of-date liquor advertisements reminding you to "Drink cool!" or "Add a splash of class!" And on the night I visited C'est la Guerre! the bar's one sad-looking jukebox in the corner was playing—I kid you not—"If I Could Turn Back Time" by Cher.

The place looked like a forgotten place.

But the décor matched the patrons, so I guess it all worked out. At my ceremonious first steps into my first gay bar, that bar had only two people in it—a bald, angry-looking bartender who never said a word to me, and Paul, a drag queen sitting alone at the bar.

I walked in and Paul took one look at me, dressed in my ill-fitting pleated khakis, a button-down shirt, and a Looney Tunes character tie, and he squealed with laughter.

"Cute, honey! Cuuuute! Come here. Come sit down. Don't just stand in the doorway. You're letting all the stink in from the garbage cans."

I sat down next to Paul and he loudly patted the torn-cushioned stool next to him.

"What are you drinking?"

"I don't know," I said. I honestly didn't. I had never ordered a drink in my life.

"I'm having a gin and tonic. So, why don't you have a gin and tonic? Then we'll have something in common."

The silent bartender made me a gin and tonic and set it down in front of me. And all of a sudden, Paul and I had something in common.

I liked Paul. He wasn't a very good drag queen. He had the saddest blond wig, teased within an inch of its life and frozen solid with so much hair spray that flies could impale themselves on an errant flyaway. He had way too much makeup that did far too little of what it was expected to do, and he wore a black sequined pantsuit with spangles and shimmer that looked like something a Golden Girl would wear out on a date. It was hard to tell how old he actually was, but he looked ancient, weathered, shipwrecked. I mean, Paul was so busted, he didn't even have a drag name. It was just "Paul."

"So honey, is this your first time here?" Paul may have been busted, but he was nice. And he could tell that I really needed someone to be nice to me. "So what brings you to our lovely establishment tonight?"

And all of a sudden it just all started to pour out of me: how I was in the closet, but some people thought I was gay, and how I had told some people, but took it back because I was scared of them telling other, wrong people, and how I was dating this girl, but she didn't know I'd ever come here, and how my parents hate gays, at least I thought they did, I assumed they did, and still I live at home, and I'm scared I'm gay and what does that mean and what do I do, please help me, please, please, please.

Poor Paul. He probably thought he'd have a quiet night at the end of the bar in C'est la Guerre! Instead, he got a frightened teenager in a dumb Looney Tunes tie with no sense of what happens next.

What did he do? He talked to me.

"I've been seeing this guy for a couple months now. He has a girlfriend, but he doesn't love her. He just feels sort of sorry for her 'cause she got pregnant. That's where all his money's going. To her. So I didn't mind paying his electric bill, you know, because he's sweet. He comes over when he can."

He asked me questions. He told me about his boyfriend troubles. About his nephews. He asked me about my friends. My job. And he gave me advice.

"You don't have to be anything you don't want to be, honey. You just be whatever you are. Okay? You gonna do that? You can't listen to the voice in your head that says you gotta hide yourself. Nobody gets nothing good if they hide themselves. Be whatever you are, honey. That's all." Then he scribbled his phone number on a napkin. "Now come on, just in case you need someone to talk to. Here. Take it."

As I folded it up and put it in my pocket, he said this: "You. Honey, I look at you, and I see myself. I do. You remind me so much of me, I can't even stand it. Seriously. I see myself in you. Now, I may not look like much right now, but I hope you at least know...you got somewhere to go. There's so much out there, honey. So much more than you even know about right now. You don't have to be me, but you also don't have to stay this version of you, either. You can go. Wherever! Whatever! You don't have to be where you are right now forever."

I never saw or spoke to Paul again after that night. But I can confidently say that my life and Paul's life turned out to be dramatically different things. But he gave me a gift that night that I have carried with me ever since.

He gave me permission to imagine a future.

If there's one thing you take away from this book, I hope you take away the belief in your future. There's something on the other side of all the questions you have, all the insecurities you battle, all the shame you feel, all the fears you face. What's on the other side is possibility. A version of you that lives confidently, bravely, and joyfully ace.

Even if you can't quite imagine that version of you right now, I can imagine it. I know that version of you exists. And I can't wait to see what you're like when you get there.

You have a future.

So listen to Paul. You've got somewhere to go.

So go.

ONE LAST THING...

One last thing before we go.

Throughout this book, I've shared two kinds of things with you: things I've experienced and things I've learned. I hope they've been helpful. And I hope I haven't bored you.

So if I have to leave you with something, on these final pages, I figure it should be something I haven't shared with you yet. So here goes.

These are things I wish for you.

I wish you happiness. Be happy with yourself. You're this unique, interesting, one-of-a-kind human. That's amazing. And maybe you're ace on top of it? Even better! That person should be happy. *You* should be happy. I wish that for you.

I wish you peace. Don't let the noise of the world get in your head. When you get caught up in the hard stuff, just take a step back, take a deep breath, and remember who you are. The negativity of the world can't touch that. It's yours. Let that be your safe harbor.

I wish you community. We don't get through this world by ourselves. We need other people. And I hope you find the most amazing people. *Your* people. The people who understand you, who support you, who make you feel connected to something larger than yourself. Love and protect them as they love and protect you.

I wish you love. And I don't just mean romantic love. (Although it's great, if that's your thing.) I wish you all the kinds of love there is, and I wish it for you in abundance. Love is another person seeing worth in who we are, even when we struggle to see it in ourselves. I want that for you, a thousand times over. So you can know, without a doubt, that who you are, as an ace person in this world, is valuable, is important, is necessary.

I wish you well. I hope we cross paths one day. I love meeting my people. But if we don't, if you and I never find ourselves close enough to shake hands and say hello, I want you to know that I'm rooting for you. I believe in who you are and what you can bring to the world. Our community is better for having you in it. So *live your life*, and know that, even when you feel completely alone, there is always at least one person on your team.

Thank you for reading this book. I am glad you're here.

ADDITIONAL RESOURCES

If you reached the end of this book and want to continue your exploration into asexuality and the asexual community, here are some excellent resources to keep you moving in the right direction.

Websites and organizations

The Asexuality Visibility & Education Network (AVEN)
www.asexuality.org
AVEN is the largest global online hub for the asexual community. They house a large archive of asexuality resources.

Aromantic-Spectrum Union for Recognition, Education, and Advocacy (AUREA)
www.aromanticism.org
AUREA works to support the aromantic community by raising awareness about aromantic people and increasing aromantic education around the world.

The Ace and Aro Advocacy Project (TAAAP)
www.taaap.org

TAAAP raises awareness of the ace and aro communities through creating and sharing ace and aro resources.

Aces and Aros

www.acesandaros.org
Aces and Aros acts as a hub for the ace and aro community, enabling and encouraging ace and aro people to get involved in their community. Aces and Aros is a project of Asexual Outreach (www.asexualoutreach. org), a non-profit organization that's building a national advocacy movement to strengthen communities and change lives.

International Asexuality Day (IAD)

www.internationalasexualityday.org
IAD is an annual global campaign to promote awareness of the identities under the asexual spectrum.

Asexuality Archive

www.asexualityarchive.com
The Asexuality Archive collects articles, advice, activism opportunities, and other resources on asexuality.

Books (non-fiction)

A Quick and Easy Guide to Asexuality by Molly Muldoon and Will Hernandez

This book is a warm, approachable and highly informative primer on asexuality. With wonderful illustrations by Hernandez and Muldoon's thoughtful and wise words, this is a great starting place for anyone thinking about asexuality.

How to Be Ace: A Memoir of Growing Up Asexual by Rebecca Burgess

This charming and insightful graphic memoir, written and illustrated by

Burgess, is a superb depiction of one ace experience. There's a lot to identify with here, and Burgess's illustrations are a delight.

The Invisible Orientation: An Introduction to Asexuality by Julie Sondra Decker

This was a highly influential book for me at the start of my ace journey. Decker's book is one of the best books on asexuality out there, digging deeper into many of the ideas I have presented here. This book helped me understand myself, and it is an invaluable resource.

Ace: What Asexuality Reveals About Desire, Society, and the Meaning of Sex by Angela Chen

If you're ready to go beyond the basics of asexuality and explore deeper the connections between asexuality and the world, Chen's book is what you're looking for. It's a fantastic look at what asexuality teaches us about ourselves and the world around us.

Refusing Compulsory Sexuality: A Black Asexual Lens on Our Sex-Obsessed Culture by Sherronda J. Brown

Brown is one of the community's most important voices, and this book, a Black, queer feminist exploration of asexuality, is an important read. If you want to deepen the way you think about asexuality and the cultural norms it questions, this is a book for you.

Books (fiction)

The books below all contain ace or aro characters, and many are written by ace or aro writers.

The Reckless Kind by Carly Heath
The Bone People by Keri Hulme
Let's Talk About Love by Claire Kann
How To Be a Normal Person by T. J. Klune
Not Your Backup by C. B. Lee

Every Heart a Doorway by Seanan McGuire
Loveless by Alice Oseman
Beyond the Black Door by A. M. Strickland
Tarnished Are the Stars by Rosiee Thor

Ace activists and educators to follow

These folks are some of the important voices in ace activism and education. They're great resources. All of the activists and educators below can be found across many platforms, including YouTube. The accounts listed below are places where they're often active, and you can connect to their other projects from there.

Yasmin Benoit (Twitter, Instagram, and TikTok: @theyasminbenoit)
Sherronda J. Brown (Twitter: @SherrondaJBrown)
Gentle Giant Ace (Twitter: @AceGentle, TikTok: @gentlegiantace93)
TheAsexualGoddess (Twitter: @AsexualGoddess)
Queer as Cat (Twitter: @queerascat)
Dr. Pragati Singh (Twitter: @Dr_PragatiSingh)
Elle Rose (Twitter: @scretladyspider)
Aubri Lancaster (Twitter: @AubriLancaster, Instagram: @acesexeducation)
Fuck Yeah Asexual (Twitter: @FYeahAsexual)
Ace Week (Twitter: @AceWeek)

Content creators to follow

Podcasts
Sounds Fake But Okay (Twitter: @soundsfakepod)
The Ace Couple (Twitter: @the_ace_couple)

YouTube
David J. Bradley (www.youtube.com/DavidJBradley)
Slice of Ace (www.youtube.com/sliceoface)

Jaiden Animations (www.youtube.com/channel/
UCGwuOnbY2wSkW8N-cghnLpA)

TikTok, Instagram, and Twitter

All of the creators below can be found across many platforms, including YouTube. The accounts listed below are places where they're often active, and you can connect to their other projects from there.

Asexual Memes (TikTok: @asexualmemes, Instagram: @asexualmemes.tiktok)
Visibly Ace (TikTok: @visibly_ace)
Oracle of Athena (TikTok: @oracleofathena)
Micah (TikTok: @ponderingtogether)
Samanta Morrison (TikTok: @samantamorrison)
Xtra (TikTok: @xtra.depresso)
Lynn Saga (Twitter: @LynnSaga)
Ace Owl (Twitter: @AsexualResearch)
Ace Chat (Instagram: @chat_ace)
Asexual Accepting (Instagram: @asexual_accepting)
æsc (Instagram: @i.put.the.ace.in.disgrace)
AsexualsNet (Twitter: @AsexualsNet)

And if you'd like to follow me and my asexuality education project, "Ace Dad Advice," here's where you can find me:

TikTok and Instagram: @acedadadvice
Twitter: @CDaigleOrians
YouTube: www.youtube.com/AceDadAdvice
Website and advice column: acedadadvice.com

INDEX